AF413274

Biblical Preaching

BIBLICAL PREACHING

An Examination of the Biblical Demand for Preaching

Robert Curry

WIPF & STOCK · Eugene, Oregon

BIBLICAL PREACHING
An Examination of the Biblical Demand for Preaching

Wipf & Stock
An Imprint of Wipf and Stock Publishers
199 W. 8th Ave., Suite 3
Eugene, OR 97401

www.wipfandstock.com

PAPERBACK ISBN: 979-8-3852-0145-7
HARDCOVER ISBN: 979-8-3852-0146-4
EBOOK ISBN: 979-8-3852-0147-1

VERSION NUMBER 12/06/23

CONTENTS

ACKNOWLEDGMENTS AND DEDICATIONS

This book is dedicated to several individuals who helped to develop my desire for preaching and who supported me in my desire to preach and to write. This book is dedicated first to my father, William Edward Curry, a gospel preacher who proclaimed the eternal truths of the Bible for five decades. He never pushed me into a life of preaching but encouraged me toward just such a task and privilege. Second, this book is dedicated to my uncle, Richard Curry, an instructor for the Memphis School of Preaching for three and a half decades and an example to me of not only the task of pulpit preaching but also the teaching of preaching in the classroom.

This book is also dedicated to Garry Hill, my best friend for the past fifty years, my roommate in college, partner in missions travel, historical adventures, and a variety of other adventures and experiences that true best friends have. This book is also dedicated to the many preachers and professors of homiletics who mentored, shaped, and formed, and encouraged me in coming to know the task of preaching as a profession, mission, and educational focus as a student, professor, and writer.

Finally, and most importantly, this book is dedicated to Dorothy Ann Curry, my wife of forty-five years. As I sought to increase my formal education in the fields of homiletics, biblical studies, and theology, she supported and encouraged me. Through her love she has offered continuous and unbiased critique of my preaching and has been by my side as I have been privileged to preach and teach for a variety of churches, teach for a variety of schools, and do seminars and workshops in a variety of settings and locations.

INTRODUCTION

Preaching is intended to do, what? To some, preaching is intended to motivate and encourage. To others, preaching is intended to educate and inform. In the minds of a few, perhaps many, preaching is expected to rebuke and exhort. In reality, preaching should be expected to do all of that. Paul Scott Wilson wrote, "In the finest sermons we feel renewed hope, stronger faith, and recommitment to mission. More simply stated, we experience God. For this reason, we claim that preaching is an event in which the congregation meets the living God."[1]

I remember many years ago an elder of a church in another state responded to the question of who would preach that coming Sunday in the absence of their preacher. He dismissed it as no issue at all and replied, "Anybody can preach." That statement, as misguided and incorrect as it is, has haunted me ever since. One might expect those unfamiliar with the church to say such a thing, perhaps even a new Christian in his or her spiritual infancy. For a shepherd of a congregation of the Lord's church to say it and believe he is correct should not be expected. To him, preaching was just making a talk. What he failed to realize is that preaching should be the result of the preparation of the sermon and the preparation of the man who will preach it.

The *American Heritage Dictionary* defines "preaching" as "to proclaim or put forth in a sermon; to advocate, especially to urge acceptance of or

---

1. Wilson, *Four Pages of the Sermon*, 20–21.

compliance with; to deliver (a sermon)."[2] While there is nothing necessarily wrong with this definition, it views preaching more or less as just speaking or addressing a religious topic to a church. Is preaching not much more than simply speaking or addressing with words? So, what is preaching, then? Any given dictionary might define it as the delivery of a sermon or religious address to an assembled group of people, typically in church. The origin of the word "preach" is from the Old French *prechier*, from the Latin *praedicare*, "proclaim," and in ecclesiastical Latin *prae*, "before," and *dicare*, "declare," and so to declare before (someone).

Paul wrote to the church in Rome about the message of salvation and indicated how they could call on the Lord if they had believed in the word, and they could believe if they had heard, and they could hear if someone would preach, and someone would preach if he had been sent (Rom 10:14–15). On the surface that passage does not necessarily offer a description of what preaching is, only how one would come to preach the word of God. The word that is rendered as "preach," however, is *kerudzosin* which is a form of *kerusso*, which means to "proclaim or publish" such as a herald[3] would do, which Paul wrote of in 1 Cor 9:27 saying, "But I discipline my body and keep it under control, lest after preaching to others I myself should be disqualified." The word is used regarding the leper cleansed by Jesus and how the man "began to talk freely about it" (Mark 1:45). In Matt 24:14 the word describes how "the gospel of the kingdom will be proclaimed throughout the whole world." So then, Paul's words in Rom 10 reveal preaching as proclamation, the heralding of the word of God.

The word perhaps usually associated with the act of preaching is *euaggelion* which indicates "glad (good) tidings" and rendered in the English Standard Version as "proclaiming" (e.g., Matt 4:23), similar in scope to *kerusso* that was just observed. In Matt 26:13 Jesus used *euaggelion* to refer to the gospel proclaimed. This same emphasis is given to the word in Acts 16:10 where Luke recorded God's call to preach the gospel in Macedonia (Acts 16:10).

Jonathan Griffiths wrote, "Preaching in the New Testament is a public declaration of God's word by a commissioned agent that stands in

---

2. Bruce, *American Heritage Dictionary*, 1385.

3. A herald is defined by Merriam-Webster as "an officer with the status of ambassador acting as official messenger between leaders especially in war; an official crier or messenger; one that conveys news or proclaims; one who promotes or advocates."

line of continuity with Old Testament prophetic ministry."[4] Two points emerge for me out of that statement. First, that preaching is a declaration of God's word. Second, that the preaching found in the New Testament was a continuation and fulfillment of the work of God's prophets in the Old Testament. Using Griffiths's words, that *continuity* expresses more than just a speech, or a public address done by a public orator. Preaching is the presentation, the sharing of the salvation history of God in the Bible. That message is good news, and so then, gospel. It is powerful, for it is about the word of God, presented by the commission of God to proclaim. It is the power behind Jesus' commission to make disciples of the nations by baptizing them in the name of the Father and of the Son and of the Holy Spirit, so that they may be obedient to all that Jesus has commanded the faithful to do (Matt 28:19–20).

So, what is my point? Preaching is not something anyone can or should do. It is not about just having something to say. It takes faith, a commitment to the study of the word, and the preparation of the inner-spiritual self to do it as the proclamation of the good news of Jesus Christ. As the preacher takes his place behind the pulpit or wherever, he does not do so upon his own authority or his own merits. He does so by the authority given to him by Jesus Christ to proclaim the message of the salvation history of God. The very purpose of preaching is to lead all who will believe to Jesus Christ through an encounter with the Word and the eternal God who is that very Word (see John 1:1, 14). As Paul wrote to the church in Thessalonica, "And we also thank God constantly for this, that when you received the word of God, which you heard from us, you accepted it not as the word of men but as it really is, the word of God, which is at work in you believers" (1 Thess 2:13).

I like Haddon Robinson's definition of preaching: "Preaching is a living process involving God, the preacher, and the congregation, and no definition can pretend to capture that dynamic. But we must attempt a working definition anyway."[5] A key to Robinson's definition is the term "a living process," indicating that preaching is dynamic, active, and fluid. No one rule guides its process and task, for each preaching event varies because of four significant elements: (1) the speaker, (2) the location, (3) the context, and (4) the culture. At the same time, however, that preaching moment must reflect a spiritually minded speaker who proclaims the

---

4. Griffiths, *Preaching in the New Testament*, 128–29.

5. Robinson, *Biblical Preaching*, 19.

very word of God in a spiritually oriented location, and all of that occurs within a spiritual context and a spiritual culture. It is a living process of spirituality, in every way.

In its place and function over the past several decades, preaching has become more of the red-headed stepchild of worship, the church, and ministry. What do I mean? In the golden age of preaching the emphasis was placed upon the message and its effect upon the massive audiences gathered to hear it. The so-called "golden age of preaching" is a term used by Robert T. Henry in his book *The Golden Age of Preaching: Men Who Moved the Masses*.[6] Henry examines the preaching of nine significant British preachers: Alexander McLaren, Robert William Dale, Henry Parry Liddon, Joseph Parker, Charles Haddon Spurgeon, Alexander Whyte, Frederick Brotherton Meyer, John Henry Jowett, and George Campbell Morgan. These men saw their sermons printed in newspapers. This golden age of the pulpit was not confined to these men or in their time. In the twentieth century men arose, and not so long ago, who, in my opinion, carried on the phenomenon such as Harry Emerson Fosdick and Billy Graham, among many others.

Preaching has evolved in a way toward the speaker rather than the message. While there are those who still appreciate a well-crafted, biblical sermon, the majority perhaps favors the popular, media preacher. The message is secondary, perhaps not even important as long as the event is glossy, flashy, and entertaining. Due to the emphasis on worship as spectacle and preaching as entertaining speech the preacher who intends to motivate, encourage, challenge, educate, inform, rebuke, and exhort has fallen into disfavor. In such a situation, such preaching is dull and lifeless.

I am reminded of the classic comedy sketch of *Mr. Bean*, portrayed by Rowan Atkinson, when he attends a worship service.[7] Once he is seated in the front pew, he quickly learns that he does not know the words to the songs (except the more familiar chorus, which he sings with enthusiasm). When the preacher begins to speak, he is heard as a droning, mumbling sound, and Mr. Bean finds it very difficult to remain awake. Perhaps without intending to do so (or perhaps with every intention), Atkinson captures

---

6. Henry, *Golden Age of Preaching*, 35.

7. *Mr. Bean* was a British sitcom created by Rowan Atkinson and Richard Curtis that began in January of 1990 and ended in December of 1995. It was developed by Atkinson, who starred as Mr. Bean, "a child in a grown man's body," who is faced with a series of humorous incidents that emerge from common, everyday tasks and experiences (Cavendish, "Atkinson," para. 3).

a rather negative perspective of preaching and in doing so reflects modern thinking, even within the minds of those in the pews.

The actual act of preaching, therefore, is considered by some as unnecessary and archaic. The preacher is no longer seen as an intellectual or spiritual leader in the congregational community, or even in secular society as well.[8] To combat such negativity, a greater emphasis has been placed, for example, on small group worship and ministry or special programs of spiritual growth.[9] Of course, there is absolutely nothing wrong with such programs and activities, for they are potentially advantageous to the spiritual health and development of a congregation.

Fred Craddock called for "a stay of execution" until all of the evidence is in.[10] Preaching that is rooted in Scripture and founded upon the gospel must be a part of the worship experience and be a catalyst for spiritual encouragement, spiritual growth, and the development. Robinson proposed, "In spite of the 'badmouthing' of preaching and preachers, no one who takes the Bible seriously dare count preaching out."[11] When done properly and biblically, preaching is challenging and awakening. It makes a connection between the text and the hearer. Robinson calls it "the event through which God works."[12]

Tom Rainer, in *Surprising Insights Among the Unchurched*, wrote that more than ninety percent of those surveyed said that preaching led them to choose a church.[13] Why might that be true? Several reasons can be listed, including the following:

1. An acceptable style: every preacher has his own style of preaching (e.g., expository; conversational) which may or may not be appealing to any given hearer.

2. A palatable message: this is an issue of articulation, how the message of the text is to be proclaimed and made to be understood.

---

8. Robinson, *Biblical Preaching*, 15.

9. I do not say this as a criticism of small group ministry or programs of spiritual growth, for each, when done biblically, offer tremendous efforts of congregational growth and development. And yet, when done at the expense of preaching much is lost. When done well, with great prayer and care, the task of preaching proves itself as a vital tool to congregational effectiveness.

10. Craddock, *As One without Authority*, 1.

11. Robinson, *Biblical Preaching*, 17.

12. Robinson, *Biblical Preaching*, 17.

13. Rainer, *Surprising Insights*, 55.

3. The use of Scripture: how much or how little reference is attributed to Scripture.

This is understandable, for every preacher, as with other types of public speakers, must understand their audience, including how they can be reached.

This is seen through two opposite styles of preaching: fire-and-brimstone and health-and-wealth preaching. The former represents a style popular in days past and still has an audience in certain geographical locations. The latter represents a style popular in media-based churches and churches with perhaps a more casual view of Christianity. Rainer's observations regarding preaching and the unchurched are on point, for they will be attracted to preaching, and so then the church overall perhaps, that appeals to their level of comfort and expectations.

Preaching then has a specific purpose. Instead of just a talk, it is intentional, planned, and declarative. It expresses the very words of God spoken to inform, persuade, and change those who hear it. Paul said it well to the church in Rome: "For I am not ashamed of the gospel, for it is the power of God for salvation to everyone who believes, to the Jew first and also to the Greek" (Rom 1:16).

CHAPTER 1

FOUNDATIONAL CONCERNS OF PREACHING

P reaching is not merely the speaking of words, but it is the proclamation of God's words. That means that there are some foundational concerns with preaching that must be addressed. Fred Craddock wrote, "Preaching beings the Scriptures forward as a living voice in the congregation. Biblical texts have a future as well as a past, and preaching seeks to fulfill that future by continuing the conversation of the text into the present."[1] I love Craddock's referral of preaching as "a living voice," for it implies that preaching has a specific dynamic that resonates among those who will proclaim the biblical text.

Preaching, then, has a specific place and function within the church. This chapter briefly discusses three of those concerns: a philosophy of preaching, a theology of preaching, and the inspiration of God's words. They form a solid foundation upon which the task and privilege of preaching functions effectively. To know and properly use that foundation is to render what preachers are to do as proclaimers of God's word.

---

1. Craddock, *Preaching*, 27.

A PHILOSOPHY OF PREACHING

Let's briefly examine a philosophy of preaching. Such a philosophy, as with any philosophy really, stems from one's worldview. "Worldview" can be understood as a fundamental cognitive orientation of an individual or society encompassing the entirety of the individual or society's knowledge and point of view, including natural philosophy; fundamental, existential, and normative postulates; or themes, values, emotions, and ethics.[2] It is derived from the German *weltanschauung* (*welt*, "world," and *anschauung*, "view or outlook"). Fundamental to German philosophy and epistemology, it refers to a wide world perception. So then, it identifies the framework of ideas and beliefs through which an individual, group, or culture interprets the world and interacts with it.

A philosophy of preaching is based on a fundamental biblical worldview rather than political, social, natural, philosophical, or other similar theories. Peter Adam, in laying down three biblical foundations of preaching, also offered a foundation for a philosophy of preaching. Adam's first foundation is "God has spoken." He comments, "God speaks, and his words are powerful, effective, and creative of reality. The God who *speaks* is the God who *acts* through his words."[3] This foundational principle is significant to understanding preaching because modern theology has developed an aversion to the idea of God speaking through his word. William Dulles, for example, asserts that biblical revelation is not the truth concerning God but the living God himself; that is revealed but not through his own words or, perhaps, even his own acts. The point centers on whether God actually has spoken when he is said to speak in the text. Preaching is either a proclamation of how we see him to be, or what he says about himself in the text.

Adam's second foundational philosophy of preaching is "it is written," which takes the first foundational point a step further. Specifically, it implies that not only did God speak for himself, and so revealed himself, but he preserved his words for mankind to read, study, and know. So then, Isaiah wrote, "And now, go, write it before them on a tablet and inscribe it in a book, that it may be for the time to come as a witness forever" (Isa 30:8). In Hab 2:2–3 the prophet wrote, "And the Lord answered me: 'Write the vision; make it plain on tablets, so he may run who reads it. For still the vision awaits its appointed time; it hastens to the end—it will not lie. If it

---

2. Palmer, *Toward a Theory*, 114.

3. Adam, *Speaking God's Words*, 15.

seems slow, wait for it; it will surely come; it will not delay.'" Daniel wrote, "In the first year of Darius the son of Ahasuerus, by descent a Mede, who was made king over the realm of the Chaldeans—in the first year of his reign, I, Daniel, perceived in the books the number of years that, according to the word of the Lord to Jeremiah the prophet, must pass before the end of the desolations of Jerusalem, namely, seventy years" (Dan 9:1-2). The apostle Paul wrote to the church in Rome regarding the authority of God: "For it is written, 'As I live, says the Lord, every knee shall bow to me, and every tongue shall confess to God.' So, then each of us will give an account of himself to God" (Rom 14:11-12). This is a significant point of preaching, for it is intended to be formed and proclaimed from the biblical text. So, part of a philosophy of preaching is its grounding in Scripture.

Adam's third foundational philosophy of preaching is "preach the word" which implies that not only has God spoken his words and has preserved his words in writing, but that we have a commission to preach his words. This point demands that God's word is to be spoken, presented for the edification and the learning of the hearer.

Moses is a good example of four significant points of a philosophy of preaching. First, Moses spoke for God. In Exod 20:18–19 and 34:34 we read, "Now when all the people saw the thunder and the flashes of lightning and the sound of the trumpet and the mountain smoking, the people were afraid and trembled, and they stood far off and said to Moses, 'You speak to us, and we will listen; but do not let God speak to us, lest we die. . . .' Whenever Moses went in before the Lord to speak with him, he would remove the veil, until he came out. And when he came out and told the people of Israel what he was commanded.'"

Second, Moses wrote down God's words. In Exod 24:4 we read, "And Moses wrote down all the words of the Lord. He rose early in the morning and built an altar at the foot of the mountain, and twelve pillars, according to the twelve tribes of Israel." In Deut 27:2, 8, the text states, "And on the day you cross over the Jordan to the land that the Lord your God is giving you, you shall set up large stones and plaster them with plaster. . . . And you shall write on the stones all the words of this law very plainly."

Third, Moses read God's words. Exodus 24:7 states, "Then he took the Book of the Covenant and read it in the hearing of the people. And they said, "'All that the Lord has spoken we will do, and we will be obedient.'" In Deut 31:30 and 32:44 it was written, "Then Moses spoke the words of this song until they were finished, in the ears of all the assembly of Israel. . . . Moses came and recited all the words of this song in the hearing of the people, he and Joshua the son of Nun."

Fourth, Moses preached Gods words. In Deut 1:5 we read, "Beyond the Jordan, in the land of Moab, Moses undertook to explain this law, saying. . ." In Deut 5:1–21 Moses offered the Ten Commandments to the children of Israel, revealing the will of God. In Deut 29 Moses offered a renewal of the covenant, a restatement in a way of the laws and commands of God. These and so many other examples indicate how the spoken word played a vital role in the mission of Moses to the children of Israel.

A philosophy of preaching must be centered on God and his word, as well as his purpose. I am reminded of Isa 61:1–2 where the prophet explained how "the messianic servant,"[4] which is fulfilled in Jesus Christ, proclaimed, "The Spirit of the Lord God is upon me, because the Lord has anointed me to bring good news to the poor; he has sent me to bind up the broken hearted, to proclaim liberty to the captives, and the opening of the prison to those who are bound; to proclaim the year of the Lord's favor, and the day of vengeance of our God; to comfort all who mourn." The Messiah himself, anointed to bring good news, preached the liberation of a new people through the redemption of God.

In a philosophy of preaching, the word of God is at center stage. While such a statement seems to reveal what is obvious, preaching may or may not express such a theocentric philosophy. Instead, a form of preaching emerged some time ago that was more about the wants and desires of both the preacher and the audience. Biblical preaching must bear a philosophy that places God and his word at the very core of the message.

A THEOLOGY OF PREACHING

If one were to peruse the vast list of books addressing the task of preaching, a variety of topics would be discovered:

1. The preparation and delivery of sermons

2. Biblical exegesis

3. Assessments of modern preaching

4. Various histories of preaching

4. Dennis and Grudem, *ESV Study Bible*, 1352.

Included in some of these books would be a chapter or more addressing a theology of preaching. In fact, entire books are sometimes entitled as a theology of preaching, but too often they are little more than examinations of one or more of the topics just mentioned. To be sure, when the air has cleared, and the dust has settled, relatively little time is devoted to what a theology of preaching really is.

A theology of preaching is the framework upon which proper exegesis and interpretation is to be hung. It is the biblical foundation that must inform and drive the task of sound biblical preaching that seeks the message of the gospel. It is discernible and can be stated by the following assertions.

The Centrality of God

It should be a given that God is at the center of the Christian's faith (e.g., 1 Pet 1:21). Examples abound of those who have removed God from the equation, relying instead upon human devices and machinations. In mankind's quest for a self-defined sense of spiritual authenticity God as sovereign Lord (*adonai*) has been pushed aside to be replaced by what is more socially acceptable; something more palatable to the spiritually errant. The fact of the matter is, however, that all we do and say in worship and life must be pleasing to such a sovereign God, for he is the one and only God. Hezekiah stated this with certainty in his prayer: "O Lord God of hosts, God of Israel, enthroned above the cherubim, you are the God, you alone, of all the kingdoms of the earth; you have made heaven and earth" (Isa 37:16).

Preaching, if it will be biblical, must be shaped by our acknowledgement of God as the one and only God; the one before whom we bow. We are the covenanted people of God, and we must approach him with his covenantal language in mind: "And I will be their God, and they shall be my people" said the prophet (Jer 31:33). Preaching must express such a relationship. We are the people of God, and it is to him we offer our lives and our worship. If God is not at the center of our faith and living, then our preaching cannot be biblical or acceptable. A theology of preaching begins there.

A High View of Scripture

As Paul stated clearly, "All Scripture is given by inspiration of God, and is profitable for doctrine, for reproof, for correction, for instruction in righteousness, that the man of God may be complete, thoroughly equipped for every good work" (2 Tim 3:16–17 NKJV). Just as God must be central and sovereign to our lives, his word must be central as well. Scripture must be acknowledged as divinely inspired and capable of making us the servants God commands us to be.

This must be especially true in biblical preaching, for God's word forms the foundation upon which preaching is done and from which the message of preaching is derived. As a proclaimer of the biblical message the preacher is a herald (*kerux*), and his task is clear and straightforward: he is to proclaim the divinely-inspired word to the world in need of salvation. This is not the foregone conclusion one might assume, for biblical preaching should logically be biblically based, but too often this is not the case. Modern society has been lulled by the spectacle of the *big preacher* and the *big church* where the emphasis is not on the gospel message, but on the showmanship of the organization. Many examples of just such a phenomenon exist. There is more about the speaker than about the Lord; there is more about the organization than about the foundation of Scripture. You have heard it said before, but it is true, nonetheless. It is about the message proclaimed and not about the proclaimer of the message. It is about the eternal message, not the mortal man.

In a theology of preaching God's truth must be paramount and the Bible must be the only source for such truth. In the "happiness" preaching that permeates pulpits across the nation, this theological foundation is forgotten. The covenant relationship of God and mankind, the reality of sin and its result, the glory of the distinctive church of the New Testament, and the relevance of true spirituality are sadly neglected, for they are not popular topics.

In such settings a high view of Scripture is fading, if not nonexistent. A high view of Scripture believes the Bible is relevant for the modern audience. Within its narratives, Epistles, and historical accounts is the information necessary for one to live justly before God. A theology of preaching accepts the Bible as the authoritative word of God.

Bringing the Hearer to a Decision

Preaching must have a purpose, not only in worship but in spiritual life as well. The preacher must know why he is proclaiming the word of God; why the time is taken to profess the gospel to all who will hear it. Again, Paul stated it well: "I charge you in the presence of God and of Christ Jesus, who is to judge the living and the dead, and by his appearing and his kingdom: preach the word; be ready in season and out of season; reprove, rebuke, and exhort, with complete patience and teaching" (2 Tim 4:1–2). Preaching is intended to proclaim the truth of the gospel message and then to encourage all who will hear it to respond to its expectations.

Preaching seeks to bring the hearer to a decision. God confronts the unbeliever, the rebellious, and the erring through the preaching of his word. Biblical preaching demands change. Biblical preaching demands improvement. This is implied in the words of Peter at Pentecost where he encouraged them to "hear these words" and then challenged them to "know for certain that God has made him both Lord and Christ, this Jesus whom you crucified" (Acts 2:22, 36). Peter expected them to decide what they would do with Jesus, who is Lord. In the Old Testament Joshua challenged the tribes of Israel to choose that day whom they would serve: the gods of their fathers, the gods of the Amorites, or the true God of Israel (Josh 24:15). Joshua's choice that he and his household would serve the Lord was an example of Israel's need to decide.

The truth is not preached without the expectation of a choice to be made. Preaching is not intended to merely be a lecture on certain facts. That is for the classroom, not the pulpit! In a theology of preaching there is a clear expectation of a decision.

THE INSPIRATION AND AUTHORITY OF THE BIBLE

In 2000 I spent several weeks with individuals who claimed a level of Christianity. They were religion majors at a well-known university, but there was little evidence of moral, Christian living, nor any desire for such. They were thrilled by biblical stories and "church song" singing, however, asking my friends and I to sing another song or tell that Bible story again. I was sitting with a few of them one night looking into the Judean night sky. As I sat amazed at the scene, I said, "The heavens declare the glory of God." They looked at me and asked me to repeat what I had said, which I did. "Where did you hear that?" they replied. I told them that it is the beginning of Ps 19. I then referred to Ps 8:1 and the psalmist's amazement at the majesty of the name of God and the glory of the heavens. They were not familiar with such things. I was drawn to these people, for they were searching for something they could not identify, but in all of the wrong places. To them, the Bible was a great collection of fictitious or altered stories with little application to real life.

Anyone who travels within the general religious world can see a vast change in respect for the Bible. While the Bible is still popular and it is read, taught, and preached throughout the world, it is not respected. What do I mean? The Bible is considered to be a good and even great source of information, yet there are many who do not believe in its divine inspiration. In other words, it is in the hands of many, even most, but the reactions range from a general disassociation and apathy toward it, its acceptance as a guide for life but not a mandate for change, and a strict, literal adherence to its authority.

To determine the Bible's origin is to determine its purpose and relevance. This book claims the Bible to be divinely inspired, an eternal gift from God. It must be, or it is a lie. Why do I say that? I say that because it claims to be inspired. Paul, in 2 Tim 3:16–17, wrote, "All Scripture is breathed out by God and profitable for teaching, for reproof, for correction, and for training in righteousness, that the man of God may be complete, equipped for every good work." The word rendered "inspired" is rendered from the Greek *theopneustos* which implies the "breath of God." The point of that is the Bible is what has come out of the mouth of God, what he has "breathed" upon us. You see, the Bible must be divinely inspired because it claims to be and if it is not, then it, all of it, is a lie. It is not a lie, however, for it is the words of God and the very epitome of truth. Paul wrote to the churches in Galatia of the "truth of the Gospel" (Gal 2:5). He encouraged Timothy and the Ephesian church to handle properly "the word of truth" (2 Tim 2:15).

Knowing the divine inspiration of the Bible demands that God comes first in all things. Israel had a problem with this. In Josh 20:14–15 Joshua challenged the children of Israel to make a choice:

> Now therefore fear the Lord and serve him in sincerity and in faithfulness. Put away the gods that your fathers served beyond the River and in Egypt, and serve the Lord. And if it is evil in your eyes to serve the Lord, choose this day whom you will serve, whether the gods your fathers served in the region beyond the River, or the gods of the Amorites in whose land you dwell. But as for me and my house, we will serve the Lord.

Israel's entire history was about swaying back-and-forth. The prophet Elijah asked, "How long will you go limping between two different opinions? If the

Lord is God, follow him; but if Baal, then follow him" (1 Kgs 18:21). Baal was an appealing god to them and that, in part, is why they struggled. So, Jeroboam, the tenth century king of Israel,[5] set up golden calves for worship at Bethel and Dan (1 Kgs 12:29), and Jehu, a ninth century king of Israel, refused to remove them at God's command (2 Kgs 10:28–29).

Jesus focused his ministry on putting God first in all things. So, he instructed the multitude to "seek first the kingdom of God and His righteousness" (Matt 6:33). Later in his ministry, Jesus responded to the inquiry of the Pharisees that the greatest commandment in the Law was to love God with all of one's soul, heart, and mind (Matt 22:37-38). The inspiration and authority of the Bible demand this, for a lack of respect for the Bible means God is replaced, that he is secondary. Consider Matt 16:26 where Jesus asked his disciples, "For what will it profit a man if he gains the whole world and forfeits his soul? Or what shall a man give in return for his soul?" Respect for biblical inspiration and authority makes Jesus' question and challenge resonate. It reminds me of Jesus' warning against building a house on the sand (Matt 7:24–27). Without God and biblical authority there is nothing truly worthwhile, even though one can build on unstable sand. Putting God and all that he represents first demands the stability of rock not sand (see Matt 7:24–27). God and his authority, through his divine word, must come first.

Knowing the divine inspiration of the Bible also demands that the Bible be accepted just as it is. Just imagine if other authoritative and informative books were handled as is the Bible. For example, the *Oxford Illustrated American Dictionary*[6] (or another authoritative dictionary) is accepted as the authority on how words are defined and spelled. Through its authority the dictionary becomes the final word. Yet, if Webster's Dictionary is disrespected as the Bible is disrespected, response to it would vary. One might say, "Well, you spell that word how you want, and I will spell it how I want." Another might respond, "Well, that is what it means to you, but not to me." Consider the educational chaos if the dictionary were treated in the same way as the Bible. Spelling tests and spelling bees would be irrelevant, research papers would be nonsense, and instruction sheets would

---

5. Israel was divided by this time into Judah (including kings such as Rehoboam, Joash, Hezekiah, and Josiah) and Israel (including kings such as Zimri, Ahab, Jehu, and Pekah).

6. Jewell and Abate, *Oxford Illustrated American Dictionary*.

be unreadable. Our dictionaries, however, are the authority for definition and spelling because society cares about such things.

The Bible must be respected and loved as the very word of God, and it is unchangeable. Consider Heb 13:8, which clearly proclaims Jesus to be the same yesterday, today, and tomorrow. Since Jesus is the Word (John 1:1, 14), the word of God is the same yesterday, today, and tomorrow. It is the same through the ages and it does not change, it does not grow old and archaic, and it will not and cannot be replaced. Peter's response to those gathered at Pentecost and asked what they must do for their salvation (Acts 2:38) is just as viable today as it was when he spoke the words. Paul's warning of the unrighteousness of the world (Rom 1:18–32) is just as true today and then. Jesus' promise of "a place prepared" (John 14:1–6) is still thrilling and comforting to all who will hear and believe it. The Hebrews writer's warning of falling into the hands of the living God (Heb 10:31) is still a warning today.

Why is the Bible to be respected? It bears the very signature of God: his inspiration, his authority, his power, and his will. How can anything with God's signature on it be less than eternal? How can it ever be replaced? How can it ever receive anything less than our utmost trust and respect? In a time when the world is drowning in its own ineptitude, the Bible must be the source of all that is good and hopeful. In a time when Christianity is merely a suggestion to too many and faith and hope are merely relative terms, the inspiration and authority of the Bible is paramount, for God's fingerprints are all over it.

Biblical preaching is concerned with the Bible, for it is at the very center of what preaching is intended to do: proclaim the truth that can only come from God who is at the very center of the Bible's authority and relevance. A philosophy of preaching and the theology behind it revolves around God. Preaching is intended to bring the hearer of its message to a decision about God, his word, and promise of eternal salvation. All of that is founded upon one very dynamic reality: Scripture is the breathed-out word of God.

CHAPTER 2

THE BIBLICAL DEMAND FOR PREACHING

Perhaps it is a bit of a given for a preacher to insist upon the importance of preaching. It is a bit like an athlete describing the thrill of sports or a scientist explaining the joy of discovery. To be sure, a lot of information has been printed regarding what preaching is and is not, what it is intended and not intended to be, and how it fits into the climate of every congregation. All of that is well and good, but for some reason the place and function of preaching is still a bit lost in the minds of some in the pews and, sadly, in the minds of some in the pulpit.

In 2 Tim 4:1–5 Paul instructed and encouraged Timothy regarding the place and function of biblical preaching:

> I charge you in the presence of God and of Christ Jesus, who is to judge the living and the dead, and by his appearing and his kingdom: preach the word; be ready in season and out of season; reprove, rebuke, and exhort, with complete patience and teaching. For the time is coming when people will not endure sound teaching, but having itching ears they will accumulate for themselves teachers to suit their own passions and will turn away from listening to the truth and wander off into myths. As for you, always

be sober-minded, endure suffering, do the work of an evangelist, fulfill your ministry.

While this is by no means the definitive description of the function of preaching, for the purposes of this chapter in this book, it offers a solid foundation. Timothy was perhaps subject to "fear," which is rendered from the Greek, *deilia*. It was used in non-biblical literature to describe those who fled the battlefield in fear. So perhaps Timothy faced times of timidity, even cowardice in his preaching (cf. 1:6–7), so Paul felt the need to encourage him to preach boldly. Paul was only too aware of the incredible need for biblical preaching and encouraged his younger friend and brother in Christ, Timothy, to take every opportunity ("be ready in season and out of season," 2 Tim 4:2) to preach the truth through reproof, rebuke, and exhortation. The reason for Paul's urgency is his knowledge that the day was soon coming when many would reject the truth of the Bible and turn to preaching that suited them ("itching ears").

A note in the *ESV Study Bible* refers to Paul's words as "the ultimate charge."[1] While that may be a bit overstated, it does place a significant flag on the passage and words within it. Paul is concerned about the future of preaching and Timothy's place within it. For Paul, preaching was intended to accomplish three essential tasks: reprove, rebuke, and exhort the audience with the truth of the Scriptures because the day was approaching when such proclamation will no longer be welcome (2 Tim 4:2).

Of course, Paul's warnings have proven true. Pulpits across our nation and throughout the world too often proclaim only the things people wish to hear. Paul warned Galatia of this, indicating that such was accursed (Gal 1:9). Such preaching condemns what God does not condemn, and embraces what God proclaims as disobedience. If they want constant and incessant fire and brimstone preaching, it can be found. If they want wishy-washy, socially correct preaching, it is out there. Paul demanded the better of Timothy because the Lord demands more of all who proclaim his word!

Why would preaching the truth of the Bible be something of controversy? This same urgency for biblical preaching is expressed elsewhere within the New Testament. John the Baptist prepared the way for Jesus Christ as "he preached good news to the people" (Luke 3:18). In writing his Epistle to the church in Rome, Paul told them, "So I am eager to preach the gospel to you also who are in Rome" (Rom 1:15). Later in that same Epistle, Paul expressed the proclamation of the salvation message

1. Dennis and Grudem, *ESV Study Bible*, 2342.

to all who would hear and believe it. He did this by expressing the reaction to the biblical message through belief and the confession of the Lord, "for everyone who calls upon the name of the Lord will be saved" (Rom 10:13). How will this happen, however? Paul explained the process as calling upon the one in whom we can believe (Jesus Christ), believing the truth because we have heard it, hearing the word of God because it is preached, and it is preached because there are those who have been sent out to preach the word of God (Rom 10:14–15).

From these examples and so many more that could be cited, we can see without doubt that biblical preaching was important to those of the first century church. Preaching should be just as important to us today, but sadly that is not the case. For whatever reason, we have come to place the donkey before the cart. Yes, I realize that is a very old analogy, but it is still relevant to the point. What is the implication of that analogy? Logic demands that to form an effective working model, the donkey (or horse or cow) must be placed in front of the cart to pull rather than push the cart. In the same way, modern thinking has placed the needs of the audience before the expectations of the Bible. In other words, instead of the Bible forming the path to preaching to the audience, it is the audience who sets the standards of what biblical preaching should be.

REIGNITING THE FIRE OF PREACHING

A specific type of preaching has been associated with "fire" for quite some time. Of course, we are all familiar with the description of preaching as "fire and brimstone," often associated with the eighteenth century American colonial preachers such as Cotton and Increase Mather, George Whitefield, and others. Such confrontational preaching is best symbolized perhaps by the sermon of Jonathan Edwards, "Sinners in the Hands of an Angry God" that frightened and mesmerized the audience with the image of God dangling the sinner over the fire as a spider might perilously hang by a web over the flames in a fireplace. In a previous time in conservative, American preaching, an especially driven and pointed sermon intended to turn hardened hearts around might have been proclaimed as "a fiery sermon."

Is a "fire and brimstone" sermon indicative of putting fire into one's preaching? Is fiery preaching more effective and even more biblical than its milder counterpart? To some it was and still is, while to others it is not and perhaps never was. The answer lies primarily in the mindset of both preacher and audience. In the days of the Edwards, the Mathers, and the Whitefields, such proclamation was part of the authoritative and confrontational sixteenth, eighteenth, and nineteenth century European and American culture of preaching which focused on sin and divine judgment.

In modern homiletical thinking, preaching has taken a dramatic turn away from anything confrontational, especially if the preacher has the unmitigated gall to warn the audience of the threat and reality of sin. Sin? Oh, I think not! And yet, in spite of such a growing trend, the fire of preaching is still a somewhat hot topic (pun intended). So how do we retrieve the fire of preaching week after week? What is that fire and how do we identify it? Should we seek to have fire in our preaching or are we expected to merely offer a homily and move on?

God, through Jeremiah, said, "Is My word like fire . . . and like a hammer that breaks the rock in pieces?" (Jer 23:29). Anyone familiar with Jeremiah's prophetic work can appreciate the force that was the word of God to a rebellious people. Perhaps that is similar to our own feelings, homileticians, on any given Monday following our preaching the previous day. We sought to bring the eternal word of God with passion and conviction, seeking to enliven, empower, and equip our congregations with a sort of spiritual fire to make it through the coming week.

The fire of preaching is not the fire-and-brimstone variety, per se, although I believe that force and spiritual accusation has its place at times. The fire of preaching is about the commitment, the conviction of the word proclaimed. It is recognizing the life-altering, hope-bringing power and authority of the gospel message. It is about telling the truth, rather than what everyone finds comfortable and appealing (see 2 Tim 4:2–4).

Let me offer two suggestions on how to rekindle the fire that should be a part of our preaching, homileticians. First, seek to interrupt the congregation. Have you ever heard of the term "wake-up call"? Of course, you have. Taken from the imagery of an alarm clock, it indicates something that had unexpectedly occurred that made us alert to something important. Effective preaching should offer a wake-up call, an alert to something vital and significant. Peter did this in the sermon at Pentecost (Acts 2). In the midst of alluding to the prophet Joel he suddenly moved the audience toward Jesus: attested by God and resurrected Jesus (while David remains in his tomb) and then added that they, the audience had crucified the Lord and Christ (36). So then, homileticians, to put some fire into your preaching, interrupt the perceptions and inclinations of your audience.

Second, move your now interrupted audience into a place of calm and security. The wake-up call should be followed by the means to embrace the reality of such alarming awakening. Again, Peter did this in the Pentecost sermon. Once he had stunned the audience with the accusation of killing the Lord and Christ (the fire), he offered them the astounding comfort of knowing how to find refuge and hope: repent, be baptized, and receive the gift of the Spirit (Acts 2:38).

One of the many things my wife and I enjoy about camping is lighting and enjoying the campfire. It invites warmth, conversation, special foods, and really relaxing times. Yet, once that time comes to leave the fire, it is good to know that it can be extinguished, rendering the campground safe. To reignite the fire of preaching is vital to effective homiletics, for it expresses a desire for the whole truth of the word and the authority it has to govern, direct, and shape all who will embrace its message.

Homileticians, perhaps it is time to reignite the fire.

The Biblical Preacher

In my opinion, to study biblical preaching is to also study the preacher, the biblical man as well. After all, it is the task of communicating God's word through the man who preaches. Recall that Paul warned the churches in Galatia of those who preach "a gospel contrary to the one you received" (Gal 1:9). Why would a preacher of God's word proclaim anything but the gospel of Jesus Christ? A study of the biblical man, the biblical preacher, is about the spirituality, the identity, and the purpose of that biblical man.

The reader will notice the photograph of a Bible. That is my Bible for preaching. You will notice that the physical condition of my Bible is rather worn and torn and scuffed. I have owned that Bible since 2008 and it has been with me throughout the United States as well as other countries. I taught the Bible and engaged in evangelistic mission work in the classrooms of a school in Tanzania as well as the front steps of houses and in the bush. That Bible was carried with me into the homes, the dirt streets, the markets, and church buildings in Peru. It has aided me in lecturing either in person or via Zoom and streaming services in four different universities associated with the churches of Christ. It has sat upon the podium where I preach and teach, as well as in similar locations in several states of our wonderful country. That Bible's worn condition is a testimony to the privileges I have had in teaching and proclaiming the word of God.

The preacher as a man is benefitted by a study of Isa 6:1-13:

> In the year that King Uzziah died I saw the Lord sitting upon a throne, high and lifted up; and the train of his robe filled the temple. Above him stood the seraphim. Each had six wings: with two he covered his face, and with two he covered his feet, and with two he flew. And one called to another and said: "Holy, holy, holy is the Lord of hosts; the whole earth is full of his glory!" And

the foundations of the thresholds shook at the voice of him who called, and the house was filled with smoke. And I said: "Woe is me! For I am lost; for I am a man of unclean lips, and I dwell in the midst of a people of unclean lips; for my eyes have seen the King, the Lord of hosts!" Then one of the seraphim flew to me, having in his hand a burning coal that he had taken with tongs from the altar. And he touched my mouth and said: "Behold, this has touched your lips; your guilt is taken away, and your sin atoned for." And I heard the voice of the Lord saying, "Whom shall I send, and who will go for us?" Then I said, "Here I am! Send me." And he said, "Go, and say to this people: Keep on hearing, but do not understand; keep on seeing, but do not perceive. Make the heart of this people dull, and their ears heavy, and blind their eyes; lest they see with their eyes, and hear with their ears, and understand with their hearts and turn and be healed." Then I said, "How long, O Lord?" And He said: "Until cities lie waste without inhabitant, and houses without people, and the land is a desolate waste, and the Lord removes people far away, and the forsaken places are many in the midst of the land. And though a tenth remains in it, it will be burned again, like a terebinth or an oak, whose stump remains when it is felled. The holy seed is its stump."

The historical setting is of that writing is c. 740 BC.[2] It occurs during the reign of King Uzziah, also called Azariah. The death of Uzziah/Azariah ended fifty-two years of national prosperity in Judah (2 Kgs 15:2–7; 2 Chr 26). He was sixteen years old when he assumed the throne (2 Chr 26:1). The chronicler wrote, "He set himself to seek God in the days of Zechariah, who instructed him in the fear of God, and as long as he sought the Lord, God made him prosper" (26:5). Later, however, he became strong and arrogant "to his destruction. For he was unfaithful to the Lord his God and entered the temple of the Lord to burn incense on the altar of incense" (26:16). Corruption and disobedience were common during the reign of Uzziah/Azariah and then Jotham. During Uzziah's reign, "the high places were not taken away. The people still sacrifice and made offerings on the high places" (2 Kgs 15:4). God struck Uzziah with leprosy, a word referring to severe skin diseases including but not limited to leprosy (19–21) and he remained a leper until his death (2 Kgs 15:5). After Uzziah's death his son Jotham, who had been his coregent for about ten years, became king. We read, "And he did what was right in the eyes of the

---

2. The dating of Isaiah's prophecy is debated with earlier and later dates suggested. That date will suffice as a ballpark figure in this study.

Lord according to all that his father Uzziah had done, except he did not enter the temple of the Lord (2 Chr 27:1). Yet, during Jotham's reign, "the people still followed corrupt practices" (2 Chr 27:2).

Isaiah places the events of Isa 6 and the supporting information in 2 Kgs 15 and 2 Chr 26 and 27 within this time frame. In a time of physical, political, and social prosperity, true spirituality was lacking. A true man of God was needed to proclaim the will of God, clearly and succinctly. Isaiah was skeptical of his task at first, claiming the inadequacy of having "unclean lips" (Isa 6:5). God cleansed Isaiah's "lips" and Isaiah arose to the task of prophecy and proclamation: "Here I am! Send me" (6:8).

The Ethos of the Preacher

Good homiletical theory involves a consideration of the man who preaches, as well as the exegetical, theological, and communicative concerns. Aristotle proposed three modes of persuasion: ethos, pathos, and logos. I will focus on ethos and leave the other two for another time and another discussion.

Ethos is the most powerful form of persuasion, which makes it a significant part of a larger theology of preaching. The point is about how the audience perceives the speaker. Is he a leader, one that others will look to for guidance and direction? Is he a man of integrity, one that can be trusted due to his honesty? Is he a man of ability who is capable to articulate the Bible in an understanding way? Is he a man known for his spirituality and his desire to walk with God?

A balance between the persuasion of the speaker and the message of the text must be formed. Otherwise, a situation similar to Corinth can arise where some followed Paul, some followed Cephas, some followed Apollos, and some followed Christ (1 Cor 1:12). The world has seen a tremendous rise in emphasis of the messenger rather than the message for the past several decades. Such an emphasis has perhaps altered the way preaching is viewed, making it about eloquence, style, and rhetoric rather than the biblical message.

Aristotle insisted that ethos is concerned with the man's character, competence, and good intentions. The ethos of the preacher is concerned with what the audience needs, wants, and expects (all three). Quintillian believed that ethos is not confined to the speaking moment, but the whole life of the speaker; that he is the "good man speaking well."[3] Andre Resner

3. Decaro, "Roman Republic," para. 12.

differentiated between "real ethos" and "perceived ethos."[4] Real ethos, he wrote, is concerned with who one really is before God and perceived ethos is concerned with how the audience perceives him. Paul had a different ethos which was not driven by audience needs or expectations, but by the message of the cross. He was concerned with the needs, wants, and expectations of the audience but all of that was shaped and formed through the message of the cross.

Why is ethos a concern? The moral and ethical questions that have arisen among preachers have illuminated gaps and quirks within the perceived work and purpose of preaching. Televangelists have been a part of American society, as well as throughout the world, for more than a century. They are charismatic speakers and have big personalities that speak before audiences of thousands around the world. Many have been seen as highly influential, highly motivated, and highly paid men and women who command the attention of a significant portion of the Christian world. Their televised worship services and, with some, their scheduled programming on television stations and now streaming services are a phenomenon.

The world of televangelism has not been bereft of moral issues, especially involving money and human relationships. Many of us can recall the arrests of some and the public confessions and shed tears of others. A counterpoint to this is that they were and are human beings prone to sin such as we read in Rom 3:23, "for all have sinned and fall short of the glory of God." First John 1:8–10 reminds us of this penchant for sin and declares that if we say we are without sin, we are liars, and the truth is not in us. That balance and counterbalance of human conduct makes the ethos of preaching very real.

Consider 1 Tim 4:6–16 and how it helps with understanding and embracing the ethos of the preacher. Paul wrote these words to his younger friend and brother in Christ:

> If you put these things before the brothers, you will be a good servant of Christ Jesus, being trained in the words of the faith and of the good doctrine that you have followed. Have nothing to do with irreverent, silly myths. Rather train yourself for godliness; for while bodily training is of some value, godliness is of value in every way, as it holds promise for the present life and also for the life to come. The saying is trustworthy and deserving of full acceptance. For to this end we toil and strive, because we have our hope set on the living God, who is the Savior of all people,

4. Resner, *Preacher and Cross*, 23–24.

especially of those who believe. Command and teach these things. Let no one despise you for your youth, but set the believers an example in speech, in conduct, in love, in faith, in purity. Until I come, devote yourself to the public reading of Scripture, to exhortation, to teaching. Do not neglect the gift you have, which was given you by prophecy when the council of elders laid their hands on you. Practice these things, immerse yourself in them, so that all may see your progress. Keep a close watch on yourself and on the teaching. Persist in this, for by so doing you will save both yourself and your hearers. (1 Tim 4:6–16)

This passage is broken into two statements regarding Timothy and his relationship to the gospel of Jesus Christ. Each of these individual statements begins with Paul instructing Timothy to teach specific truths to the church in Ephesus. In verse 6 Paul wrote, "If you put these things before the brothers, you will be a good servant of Christ Jesus, being trained in the words of the faith and of the good doctrine that you have followed."

The identity of "these things" is a bit uncertain, whether Paul is referring to what has just been said in verses 1–5 or what he has written thus far in this Epistle. Personally, I believe Paul refers to all he has written to Timothy thus far in the epistle. In 3:14–15 he wrote, "I hope to come to you soon, but I am writing these things to you so that, if I delay, you may know how one ought to behave in the household of God, which is in the church of the living God, a pillar and buttress of the truth." This pattern appears to occur again in 4:11 where Paul instructs Timothy, "Command and teach these things . . . " referring perhaps to what he wrote in verses 7–10. Again, in 5:7 Paul wrote, "Command these things as well, so that they may be without reproach," referring to what was just stated in verses 1–6. Finally, in 6:2b the apostle wrote, "Teach and urge these things," referring perhaps to what was written in 5:7–6:2a.

The thrust of 1 Tim 4:6–16, and perhaps the majority of the First Epistle, is Timothy's awareness of his place and function as the preacher for the church in Ephesus where "the focus is on how Timothy, by his teaching and lifestyle, can help the church persevere in the face of the false teaching."[5] It was in consideration of Timothy's ethos: "Let no one despise you for your youth, but set the believers an example in speech, in conduct, in love, in faith, in purity" (4:12). Through his good character, sound faith, and spirituality he would help to move the congregation in the right direction in the face of coming spiritual and moral threats.

5. Dennis and Grudem, *ESV Study Bible*, 2331.

CHAPTER 3

PREACHING AND SPIRITUAL FORMATION

Spiritual formation is often seen as a private, personal journey and such it is in part. The story of one's spiritual experiences is truly that of the individual, similar in ways to those of another, but personal, none-theless. Yet, spiritual formation is also corporate, a journey shared with others, those in the community of faith.[1] What do I mean, *community of faith*? As a community of faith spiritual formation becomes more than mere personal experience, but a shared response to a growing spirituality. If the faith community is engaged, then, in spiritual formation and such is done, in part, as an interactive process, then preaching should have an integral place in such formation as well, for it too is an interactive process of the faith community.

How can preaching function as a tool of teaching-learning and spiritual communication, and as such how does it contribute to the journey of faith development? While in some ways two different components of Christian life, the terms *spiritual formation* and *faith development* will refer to the same broad-based need that preaching can help to satisfy.

---

1. For this study the terms *community of faith* and *faith community* are the same.

FUNDAMENTAL SPIRITUAL FORMATION NEEDS OF THE CHURCH COMMUNITY

One of the basic needs of many churches is to realize the function of *community*, those who form the collective of faith and worship. Gaylord Noyce comments, "The church is an intentional, confessional community," something that is perhaps unrealized in too many churches.[2] A key thought is the act of being together, a sense of corporation, and such is lost to most who function within the boundaries of this faith community. They realize, perhaps, that they share a form of fellowship but fail to understand that such togetherness is more than physical proximity or even shared activities (e.g., a fellowship dinner). While such physicality is essential to an understanding and appreciation for *community*, there are also the dimensions of emotional, spiritual, and experiential community to be understood as well. These come into play as events of worship, pastoral issues, and educational endeavors.

Sally A. Brown insists, "Christian spiritual formation is an irreducibly *ecclesial* process. Christians are normally formed, spiritually, in the context of, and by the means of, the practices of the gathered church."[3] Her term "gathered church" is informative in that it reminds us that the faith community is assembled by choice and by design, and then the experiences of this "gathered church" are also by design. It is an intentional thing, and that intention indicates something is going on, something that cannot be done, at least not as well, privately and personally.

The church is gathered for a shared purpose that is encased within the opening of Scripture and that is where the church might realize its greatest sense of community. Scripture is essential, comforting in its presence within the assembly. It is read as devotional thought, studied in the classroom, and proclaimed from the pulpit. The comfort derived from Scripture, however, is perhaps merely its *presence* and its power to change lives, to develop faith and form a greater spirituality. The Scriptures are a sort of security blanket that brings comfort by simply being there and, as a security blanket, has very little purpose otherwise. Emphasis is given to the reading and study of Scripture, but not to its application. It is enough that it is read, but to use it as a tool of faith development is perhaps a

---

2. Noyce, *Minister as Moral Counselor*, 84.

3. Brown, "Preaching as Spiritual Formation," 27.

concept too abstract. To be moved toward such an application would be helpful in one's faith development.

Charles L. Campbell offers two aspects of the faith community that are often overlooked or, perhaps more accurately, little understood. The first is rather obvious since the assembled church is a community of *faith*. Campbell insists that faith is not only "embodied in worship and discipleship," but it is also "an acceptance of the *Credo* of the community . . . an assenting to and learning of the language of the community."[4] Through Scripture the church speaks the same language of faith, one that no one else can speak. There is a sense of security in that, for the community of faith finds solace, command, and guidance from the same source, a source that they all, as a community, listen to.

Preaching is perhaps seen as a weak link, perhaps, to this language of faith. Clyde Fant comments:

> Preaching, then appears weak because it disappears into the experience of others; it vanishes, seemingly without a trace. But this is precisely what makes preaching essential to the Christian faith. It shares a great mystery with the Incarnation; "Word become flesh," and "eternal Word become subjective words." So, preaching avoids the idolatry of fixation, the static representation of God by objects, however apt or beautiful. So, preaching allows participation by the hearer, interpretation and appropriation. It is taken up in every generation, by every individual who proclaims, not as object but as subject. It is, therefore, *open*, not closed; I may participate in this reality.[5]

Second, Campbell insists that theology is not really concerned with "individual, inner experience, but with the Scripture and language of the community."[6] In other words, both faith and theology are the language of Scripture and that is a language the spiritual community speaks. Too often, however, the church is not aware it speaks this language and that it does so as a community. To acquaint them with this reality is to assist them in filling the gap of the need to understand the community of faith. Perhaps this is why some are rejecting the notion of church or organized religion, because they are not aware of the shared community, the gathered church. They see

4. Campbell, *Preaching Jesus*, 52.

5. Fant, "What Can Preaching Do?," 5.

6. Campbell, *Preaching Jesus*, 52.

religion as something archaic and irrelevant, so they abandon what is so seemingly useless and seek other means of fulfilling their spiritual quest.[7]

So, then the idea of *church* to some is a rather negative image, one that conveys stuffy rigidity; a spiritual necessity that must be endured. This is a disturbing phenomenon, of course, because it reflects a lack of concern for and understanding of the biblical nature of the church—the assembled who are being saved (Acts 2:47; 1 Cor 1:18; 15:2)—and for the necessity of the *ekklesia*, the called together for worship and edification (Col 1:18; 1 Thess 5:11). To be sure, faith will not be developed in such an environment. The biblical reality of *church* as a spiritual community, an assembled, sharing community of faith, must be a subject of preaching.

One of the biblical images regarding the church is that of the people of God, a topic of both the Old and New Testaments. Central to this is the idea of covenant, an arrangement made between God and Abraham for a great nation (Gen 12:2). This covenant promised that God would be the God of this blessed nation and that it would be his people (Gen 17:7), a "treasured . . . kingdom of priests and a holy nation" (Exod 19:5–6). As a covenanted nation it would endure forever (2 Sam 7:16) and God will remember his covenant with his people forever (Ps 105:8).

This covenanted relationship helps Christians recognize the community of faith that is the church. Certainly, those of the first century did, for they realized their release from the bondage of sin to a renewed life (Rom 6:1–7). That renewed life is found only within those of the faith community, the body of Christ (1 Cor 12:12–31). Therefore, the church shares in a sphere of unity, the sense of being one. Such was the prayer of Jesus (John 17:11) and such was the practice of the church in the first century (Eph 4:4–6). Preaching should acknowledge the community of faith that is in a covenant relationship with God.

Challenged to Develop

Another spiritual need among many churches is a willingness to accept the challenge of spiritual formation. There is a strong desire to remain the same, to not change, which means to not grow or develop spiritually. Worship is most comfortable when it is the same as in years gone by; preaching is best received when it basically reemphasizes what everyone already knows. The general desire is to remain a spectator rather than a

---

7. Gushee and Jackson, *Preparing for Christian Ministry*, 125.

participant, to reside in a comfortable niche rather than be challenged to greater faith and spirituality. This, too, is a disturbing but growing phenomenon. It is also nothing new.

Preaching can assist in changing such attitudes, for preaching can be intentionally an educational event.[8] John Koessler writes, "In order to impact my listeners, I must first get their attention. Once I have my audience's attention, I must say something worth keeping, and say it in a way that moves them to respond."[9] Indeed, the desire for response is most essential for the preaching experience, for it implies acceptance and understanding.

Preaching must, in part, challenge the listener to stretch and move beyond comfortable boundaries, which means, to allude to the mission of the starship *Enterprise*,[10] that the listener is taking them where they have not gone before. Such responsiveness directs the spiritual pilgrim on the journey toward greater faith and spirituality. Wayne Brouwer comments:

> His thinking had been changed. He saw the world through new glasses. The structures of reality had shifted for him. It was as if the fabric of life, which at one moment had been curved by the paradigms he had taken for granted, had suddenly been reframed, and the warp and woof of his existence had been straightened out.[11]

Paul saw this happening in Athens as he attempted to widen the worldview of the Areopagites by addressing their situation through their own religious practices, namely an inscription on an idol dedicated to a god with no name (Acts 17:23). He proclaimed them to be "religious," but their practice and knowledge was incomplete and, therefore, inadequate. Brouwer comments that they had not the seen "the bigger picture, and therefore [had] limited the scope of their religion."[12] Paul's preaching instructed them and, therefore, expanded their understanding by explaining the identity of the one they "worship as unknown" (Acts 17:23) and introducing them to the theology of resurrection. Having entered into the event by demanding Paul's explanation of his teaching, they were then challenged to become

---

8. Hethcock, "Sermon as an Educational Event," 21.

9. Koessler, "View From the Pew," 20.

10. The starship *Enterprise* is the spacecraft made famous by the popular television show *Stark Trek*, and the statement "to go where no man [one] has gone before" was made in the lead-in to each episode.

11. Brouwer, "Reframing Life," 30.

12. Brouwer, "Reframing Life," 31.

hearers who needed to make a response. Some of them accepted the challenge and made the changes toward faith.

John Maxwell insists that there are levels of leadership that are contracted through preaching.[13] The first, or bottom level is the "position" level, one that merely states that the preacher has a given place, a position or title, in the church with, perhaps, little or no connection to the people of the church. The second is the "permission" level where one not only has a position or title but has also received permission from the people to enter into their lives, at least to some extent. At this point, claims Maxwell, the "walk with God" is a shared one.[14] The third is the "production" level that builds from the permission level to produce results from established relationships. Maxwell adds, "The permission level is built on relationships, while the production level is built on results."[15] At this level people respond not only because of the message, but also due to the messenger. This level is one of trust.

An association with spiritual experiences arises then at the next or fourth level. One's baptism, introduction to Christ, or whatever has occurred in one's spiritual life is associated with the preaching and influence of the preacher. Maxwell claims, "You reproduce yourself in the lives of the people, you develop people, it is a personal development type of level."[16] Every listener is at one of these levels and will respond in a way that reflects that level. That is why a sermon is preached and one will be moved to greater spirituality, while another will be moved to leave and never come back. To this Maxwell comments, "In communication, in preaching it is very important for the communicator to understand when he or she walks up in front of people that they have these different stations in life."[17]

To be challenged, then, is vital for one's spiritual formation, for without a challenge to grow and develop one will not desire to do any more than he or she has already done. One's comfort zone is threatened when pleas for further growth and knowledge are made. Yet, the church must develop spiritually, and the preacher is essential to that development. As Brouwer

13. Maxwell, "Leading through Preaching," 14.

14. Maxwell, "Leading through Preaching," 14.

15. Maxwell, "Leading through Preaching," 14.

16. Maxwell, "Leading through Preaching," 14.

17. Maxwell, "Leading through Preaching," 14.

explains, "When preaching is able to reframe life or to expand the horizons of a worldview it serves people very well."[18]

A key challenge to develop in faith is the threat of pain and suffering, a shared concept of human conditioning and an essential part of spiritual formation. Such is found in the Epistles of Peter where suffering becomes central to faith development, for according Peter, "suffering was due to their affirmation of Christian faith" and "the paradigmatic example of suffering is the cross of Christ."[19] Les Steele comments that "for Peter, suffering has the potential to shape our faith" and cites both Walter Bruggemann and James Broder for clarification. Bruggemann adds that suffering and pain then become a sort of challenge, a push in the direction of a further development of faith.[20]

When the preacher understands the threat and reality of pain, whether physical or emotional, he becomes a viable tool of faith development. Such understanding is orthopathic, a sense of right passions. Orthopathy involves a sense of self-surrender,[21] both in a denial of self and in the realization of God's movement in our lives, even within the reality of pain.

The psalmist felt the rebuke and chastening of the Lord because of his iniquities and foolishness (Ps 38:1–2, 4–5). His disobedience had brought him isolation (38:11–12).

Yet, he continually called out to the Lord (38:9–10), acknowledging his sinfulness (38:17–18), because in the Lord he found his hope (38:15). To him, in the midst of pain, the Lord was the Lord of his salvation (38:21–22). Whether day-to-day human experience or from the consequences of our own mistakes, pain and trouble can be essential building blocks of faith. When the preacher realizes this and shares in the pitfalls of the shared journey of faith, he is able to communicate that journey.

Ron Mehl, a preacher who has battled leukemia for many years, offers a valuable point:

> I believe that until a pastor comes to the realization of his own mortality, and until a man realizes he's not going to live forever, I doubt that he will live with purpose or priorities. You must come to the realization that you are dying—and I'm not trying to be morbid about it. Because I realize how critical every day is, I've

18. Brouwer, "Reframing Life," 31.

19. Steele, *On the Way*, 52.

20. Steele, *On the Way*, 52; Brueggeman, *Hope within History*, 97.

21. Steele, *On the Way*, 105.

become so serious about it that my life has become more tender, not only for my touch in the life of the church, but in my family. . . . I think I've always been tender and sensitive, but the bout with leukemia has made me realize that the redemption of time is so critical. . . . Until you face your mortality, I doubt that you will live life with a whole lot of purpose. . . . [My battle with leukemia has] greatly affected my preaching. I think those who have waded through any deep waters or faced any speed bumps understand that they slow you down and cause you to look at what you're doing, at what you're preaching, at being responsible.[22]

James Loder, in *The Transforming Moment*, speaks of "negating the negative," removing the negative result from a negative reality. Steele applies Loder's point by insisting that "when we encounter suffering, we are faced with a choice: we either resign ourselves to it and so are defeated by it, or we try somehow, through the power of the Holy Spirit, to be transformed by it."[23]

Such is the essence of being challenged to grow spiritually, to develop in faith as one moves along the Christian journey. The preacher becomes vital to this formation because he is a communicator of the will of God and teller of the many biblical life stories of those who both failed and were successful in the endeavor. Churches, as a whole, need to be willing to realize the shared journey of faith they all are on toward greater faith and spirituality. Yet, the majority fail to do so because they are not willing to be spiritually challenged.

Being challenged implies action, making a move, traveling further, growing stronger, and climbing higher. John Koessler writes, "The ultimate goal of my preaching is action, I want my listeners to be doers of the word as well as hearers. In order to facilitate their response, I must help them to see what that response looks like in their own context."[24] Preaching will be effective for faith development when preacher and congregation come together, at the same level, and move together in the challenge of spiritual formation.

Preaching must reflect a sense of orthodoxy, orthopraxy, and orthopathy as the church takes the spiritual journey. All three are vital, moving from one to the other. Les Steele, borrowing from Theodore Runyon, insists that

---

22. Duduit, "Preaching and Pain."

23. Steele, *On the Way*, 105.

24. Koessler, "A View from the Pew," 22.

"it is not enough to believe the right things, or to do the right things, or to feel the right things. Our wholistic Christian faith demands all three."[25]

To realize that Christianity is not head or heart, truth or experience, but all of these things is to realize the connection between orthodoxy, orthopraxy, and orthopathy. Without orthopathy, orthodoxy is dead, and orthopraxy is hypocritical.[26] Paul stated this very thing to Corinth, insisting that if he would speak with tongues, if he could prophesy, if his faith could move mountains, if he would give all he had to the poor, or if he were willing to give himself up to a horrible death, but do none of these things through love, he would have gained nothing (1 Cor 13:1–3). Lewis Sherrill uses three metaphors of life: a treadmill, a saga, or a pilgrimage. The treadmill is "a most dreadful existence . . . a weary grind." The saga offers a certain appeal and romance, adding "a dimension of adventure and meaning," but is overall humanistic, emphasizing the individual and shutting out God.

The pilgrimage, however, "is a life journey lived before God. It is infused with meaning no matter what the circumstances."[27] Yet, the pilgrimage itself can be frightening, for the Christian journeys as a stranger in a foreign land (Heb 11:9–10). This might be especially true of new Christians or those who are on the verge of becoming Christians. Much of what is said is new and different, and that can be rather frightening and disconcerting.

John R. W. Stott writes that "the challenge of preaching is to build a bridge between the revealed Word and the contemporary world."[28] The preacher needs to realize the threat of that journey, for it is a journey into something unknown and that involves risk, something some, perhaps most, are not willing to take. Yet, there is strength in numbers, so the journey is less intimidating when one recognizes he does not travel alone.[29] James Tozer writes:

> I make joy and hope the dominant note of my sermon. A spirit of expectation and excitement fills the sanctuary because our people believe God will work and speak. They come bearing the weight of worry and discouragement. They want to cry to release the tension

25. Steele, *On the Way*, 53.

26. Gushee and Jackson, *Preparing for Christian Ministry*, 134.

27. Gushee and Jackson, *Preparing for Christian* Ministry, 43–44.

28. Tozer, "Preaching to Reluctant Pilgrims," 22.

29. Steele, *On the Way*, 45–46.

of pent-up fear; they long to embrace life's joys. People desperately need to believe and to take courage.[30]

Preachers share in the challenge of spiritual formation. Peter Adam correctly states, "If we are servants of God and of Christ, and servants of his Word, then the call of the preacher is also to be a servant of God's people."[31] What is intriguing is that not only is the preacher a servant, but he serves not as one who is above the challenge of spiritual formation, but as one who takes the journey as well. "As ministers," writes Leigh E. Conover, "like all members of the body of Christ, we have the privilege and challenge of guiding other believers along the same path that we are also taking."[32]

This path is one of obedience and discipleship to the Lord of heaven, for Christians are called to be his obedient servants. Such orthopraxy is a theme of James, "where we find an outline of true Christian formation."[33] James emphasizes the reality of not only hearing but doing the word (Jas 1:22–26). Steele comments:

> James does not refer to physical appearance but to the quality of a person. Mere hearers may have the superficial appearance of a Christian, but they have not allowed the reality of the gospel to penetrate their lives. . .Works, or right behavior, must be the natural consequences of being true believers of the word. Works are the ethical response to God's grace in our lives.[34]

That is why James insists that "pure religion" is caring for others (1:27), for not doing so but claiming to have faith is in reality a faith that is dead.

The spiritual journey of Christianity is addressed when preachers meet the church where they are, addressing their needs and fears. Preachers too are on the journey, a pilgrimage of faith and spirituality, sharing in the fears and concerns, the victories and defeats, of that journey with those to whom we preach. This sense of orthopraxy is a theme of the non-Pauline Epistles where, as in Heb 2:10 and 12:2, "Jesus is the pioneer, author and finisher of our salvation . . . our pathfinder or trailblazer. He leads the way for the pilgrim people."[35] As fellow-pilgrims, preachers need

---

30. Tozer, "Preaching to Reluctant Pilgrims," 22.

31. Adam, *Speaking God's Words*, 130.

32. Gushee and Jackson, *Preparing for Christian Ministry*, 109.

33. Steele, *On the Way*, 47.

34. Steele, *On the Way*, 47.

35. Steele, *On the Way*, 44.

to express such orthopraxy, preaching about he who leads the way, both for me and those we serve.

Clyde Fant writes that our study and hearing of the Bible becomes a shared experience of fellow pilgrims and our experiences become much needed assistance to continue on the journey. In the Scriptures are those who asked the same questions and faced the same tears and joys.[36] Hebrews 12:1, claims Fant, offers that very comfort through an emphasis of *we* and *us*: "Therefore we also, since are surrounded by so great a cloud of witnesses, let us lay aside every weight, and the sin which so easily ensnares us, and let us run with endurance the race that is set before us."[37]

The humanity of the preacher is that of the congregation as well, for all are created in the image of God and are endowed with a nature that permeates all mankind. That nature is not the nature of God for mankind faces the challenges of sin, yet at the same time the Christian, who is human, desires to be more like God, which is the very idea of godliness (1 Tim 4:7, 8; 2 Pet 3:11). Preaching must relate the challenge shared by the preacher and congregation to live effectively as being creatures in the image of God and seeking a God likeness while constantly faced with the reality of sinfulness.[38]

Preachers must seek to express this shared journey, emphasizing the victories and defeats we all face from time-to-time. Such is a relationship of orthodoxy and orthopathy, being willing to desire what God desires, come what may, as faithful servants to his will. This takes us back to the concept of *permission* I mentioned earlier; to enter the lives of those in the church, a relationship that allows such interaction to occur.

Paul sought this sort of relationship with the churches. He wrote as a spiritual father, referring to them as his children (1 Cor 4:14; 12 Thess 2:7; etc.). Through this relationship they shared, Paul not only instructed them toward godliness (1 Thess 4:1) but shared his own life and experiences with them: "So, affectionately longing for you, we were well pleased to impart to you not only the gospel of God, but also our own lives, because you had become dear to us" (1 Thess 2:8).

That is why preaching, if it will assist in the spiritual formation of the church, must be reflective of this shared pilgrimage and not, as William Willimon writes, sermons that are "twittered away in good advice, happy

36. Fant, "What Can Preaching Do?," 6.

37. Fant, "What Can Preaching Do?," 6.

38. Gushee and Jackson, *Preparing for Christian Ministry*, 108.

assurance, or harsh intimidation."[39] Fant insists "preaching that addresses us in our own language, without the interference of contrived emotions and meaningless cliches, on matters of ultimate importance to us, will be anything but boring or irrelevant."[40]

Preachers, in their preparation of sermons, often feel moments of excitement and enlightenment that lead to the formation of the sermon. William Hethcock, in realizing this, poses a pertinent question:

> If preachers, while preparing a sermon in their studies, experience a moment of excitement that prompted the Sunday sermon, why could they not allow that journey and that moment to be the form for the sermon itself? In this way the congregation would be enabled to arrive at the same moment of excitement when they heard the sermon from the pulpit.[41]

Preaching must reflect a vision that is orthopraxic, a vision that aligns our lives with the will of God. As Jesus said, "If you love Me, you will do My commandments" (John 14:15). This sense of orthopraxy can lead to orthopathy, or "right passions," desiring what God desires. In this sense of orthopathy we express the need for trust and confidence in God and his word, or as Steele puts it, "our willingness to place our life stories within the story of God and trust God," which he calls an act of self-surrender.

The vision of the preacher, what he wishes to express to the congregation as vital to the spiritual experience of Christianity, is sometimes expressed but not received. Why is this the case? Perhaps the vision is not approached in a way that is acceptable, even believable to the congregation.

This reminds me of John Maxwell's "permission" and "production" levels of leadership, where the former is a level of trust and admission into the people's lives and the latter is a level of producing results based on the permission to do so. Maxwell adds an essential note to his levels of leadership: "Your job is not to sell your vision; your job is to sell yourself. People don't buy into vision until they buy into the leader."[42] If we do not have permission to enter the lives of the church, we will not be able to produce the desired results of faith development.

Preaching, then, must produce a means to an end, moving toward a prescribed result. What is that result, however? How do we know that the

39. William H. Willimon, *Peculiar Speech*, 54.
40. Fant, "What Can Preaching Do?" 5.
41. Hethcock, "Sermon as an Educational Event," 24–25.
42. Maxwell, "Leading through Preaching," 16.

church, including the preacher, has reached it? The question is not easily, if ever, answered, and such is the case because if the church is on a spiritual journey together is it plausible to assume all will arrive at the same time, together? No, for faith development is a joint effort made by individuals who have needs and abilities that, too, are individual. That is why the needs of the congregation are to be ascertained and met.

Of course, some may not realize what needs they have, or they might insist upon meeting needs that have little to do with spiritual formation. Preaching assists them in realizing what needs are most important, most pertinent to Christian living. James L. Street suggests "that legitimate needs are those which must be met for people to realize the ends consistent with the Christian faith."[43] The disciples of Jesus had their individual needs, but soon came to realize their greatest needs encompassed what allowed them to be men faithful to their call to evangelism. They had been instructed to deny themselves and take up their crosses to follow Jesus (Matt 16:24) and all that stood in the way of fulfilling that command would no longer matter.

Perhaps the means to an end in preaching and spiritual formation is answered best not by "Have I preached well?" but "Have I served God and Christ and have I served the people of God?"[44] As I mentioned earlier, that was the focus of Paul, to serve God and the people of God (2 Cor 4:2). To Paul, orthodoxy was essential. "Scattered throughout Paul writings," writes Steele, "are teachings on the orthodox views of Christ's nature, the resurrection, and the work of the Holy Spirit. For Paul, to be about the business of Christian formation, you must be concerned with orthodox belief."[45]

Preaching, then, is not the end itself, but merely part of the means to that end, the way to reach the proper destination, and the destination is God and an observance of his will. As Street writes, "Such preaching requires that preachers always hold some well-articulated end that they are striving to meet in the sermon. For me, that end is leading people to the worship of God through Jesus Christ."[46] That is why the gospel must be key to preaching toward faith development. Steve Harper, in citing the preaching and spiritual outlook of John Wesley, writes, "People must have access to the total gospel if they are to grow properly in their faith. [Wesley's] desire is 'to describe the true, the scriptural, experimental

43. Street, "Preaching and Discerning Human Need," 31.
44. Adams, *Speaking God's Words*, 125.
45. Steele, *On the Way*, 37.
46. Street, "Preaching and Discerning Human Need," 32.

religion, so as to omit nothing which is a real part thereof, and to add nothing thereto which is not.'"

In these words, he reveals his conviction that nurture must take place in the context of an awareness of the full gospel. Here is an important insight when contrasted with a piecemeal approach, or worse, a temptation in preaching to emphasize a "pet" theme at the expense of the whole counsel of God. It is another indication that Wesley consciously selected and ordered the sermons to be spiritual formation documents.[47]

Preaching, then, to be faith developing, must reflect a desire to hear God's voice and not my own. George Carey relates the newspaper accounts of the dwindling numbers of wild birds in London due to the females not being able to hear the songs of the males over the noise of the city. He then comments: "Human beings too are often unable to hear the call of God because of all the sounds around that distract us from hearing Him."[48] As a fellow pilgrim, the preacher needs to hear that voice and share in the hearing with those who have assembled in the presence of God. If the preacher expresses a distancing away from the church, as if he is excused from the responsibilities of the assembly, preaching cannot be that means to a proper end.

Willimon writes that the "aim of evangelical preaching is . . . transformation."[49] Such transformation is done through the sharing of the gospel together, preacher and congregation, sharing in the journey of discovery. Preaching relates a story of spiritual formation. The preacher and the audience can relate to that story for they, too, have a story to tell, a story that continually unfolding. In telling the story the hearer is led to a climax, a homiletical moment that is intended to instruct, to guide, and to encourage.

47. Harper, "Wesley's Sermons as Spiritual Formation," 133–34.

48. Carey, "Spiritual Life of the Preacher," 3.

49. Willimon, *Peculiar Speech*, 55.

CHAPTER 4

PREACHING THE PARABLES

A Genre of Biblical Preaching

Now that I have addressed some of the concerns of biblical preaching, in this chapter I will observe the parables of Jesus as an example of and genre for preaching. I chose to use the parables of Jesus for two reasons: first, because of my love for the study and preaching of the parable of Jesus, and second, because the parables offer some challenges as well as great rewards when they are studied and preached. The decision to use the parables of Jesus as examples of biblical preaching did not come easily, for there are a large number of biblical genres that would be challenging and rewarding, as well, including

1. the preaching of Jesus, of course;

2. the proclamations of the prophets such as Isaiah, Amos, Joel, and so many others; and

3. the preaching of Paul in a wide variety of settings throughout his missionary journeys.

Parables are preached because they are familiar. One author insists they are "audience friendly," even easily understood and remembered.[1] It might be assumed by some then that parables are easily proclaimed. Yet is that a valid assumption? Mike Graves concedes that the parables of Jesus might be "preacher friendly" but hastens to add that their apparent simplicity and familiarity are deceptive and "can be a hindrance rather than an asset to the interpreter and preacher alike."[2]

Since the turn of the nineteenth century, much has been added to literature on the parables. Based upon the foundations laid by men such as A. B. Brice and D. Adolf Jülicher, the study of the parables of Jesus has been enriched through the scholarship of C. H. Dodd, Joachim Jeremias, A. M. Hunter, Craig L. Blomberg, Dominic Crossan, David Buttrick, and others. John R. Donahue comments, "There [is] no dearth of excellent studies of the parables" and then adds, "Yet the parables, like all great literary and artistic works, are ever old and ever new and resist capture by any one movement or period, not to say by any one book."[3]

What is a parable and how does it function? When done properly, offering a definition of a parable is no easy task for fear of omitting some of its distinctive marks or adding something superfluous. So how then is a parable defined? C. H. Dodd's definition is classic: "At its simplest the parable is a metaphor or simile drawn from nature or common life, arresting the hearer by its vividness or strangeness, and leaving the mind in sufficient doubt about its precise application to tease it into active thought."[4]

The power or force contained within a parable is found in its aesthetic value, a living quality that reaches out to the reader. The parables reflect much of Jesus' ministry: the "good news," the eschatological nature of his preaching, his call to repentance, and his conflict with the Jewish leadership. The parables are what characterized the teaching of Jesus, for they reveal the mind and historical situation of Jesus. The parables moved the reader toward the kingdom of God.

How are the parables to be preached? What is the preaching of a parable intended to do? In reality, preaching a parable can be a daunting task and its proclamation is not easily done. Thomas Long writes, "Preaching on a parable is a novice preacher's dream but often an experienced

---

1. Thielman, "Preaching the Parables," 27.
2. Graves, *Sermon as Symphony*, 40.
3. Donahue, "Jesus as the Parable," 380.
4. Dodd, *Parables of the Kingdom*, 16.

preacher's nightmare."[5] The problem is the parables appear at first to be ideal for preaching, but eventually the preacher realizes that the parables are multi-layered and rich in meaning. Craig Blomberg alludes to Colin Morris's warning that the preacher must be sure "to not do badly what the Bible has already done well,"[6] lengthening what Jesus accomplished within a few short sentences.

Some parables express a point that can be shocking and evocative, for they purposefully alter the worldview of the listener. Eugene Lowry insists that to not preach the parables is to "avoid some of the richest treasures the Bible has to offer for our preaching."[7] The parables are, according to A. B. Brice, "so large, so peculiar, and so precious a portion of Christ's teaching" they must be proclaimed. Yet, the homiletical waters have been made rather murky due in part to the variety of methods utilized. Over the decades the parables have been allegorized, psychologized, and reduced to "pointed 'lessons' on moral behavior."[8] There is little wonder that the method of preaching the parables needs further exploration.

This chapter is based on Thomas Long's three categories of parables, identified as "code," "vessels," or "objects of art."[9] According to Long "code" assumes a hidden message concealed in the text, requiring the "secret key" to the code. The "vessel" assumes the parable contains one central point and that point must be determined. The "object of art" seeks to bring the reader into the world of the parable "through identification with one of the characters of the parable or through a powerful set of images."[10]

I am very well aware, of course, that there are a variety of excellent books regarding the perspectives and discussions of the parables of Jesus, some of which will be cited in this chapter. There are also some excellent books specifically focused on preaching the parables, including *Speaking Parables: A Homiletic Guide* (David Buttrick) and *How to Preach a Parable* (Eugene Lowry). Of course, there many more journal articles on the subject, including "Preaching the Parables: Preserving Three Main Points" (in *Perspectives in Religious Studies* 11, Spring 1984, by Craig Blomberg), "Preaching the Parables and the Main Idea" (in *The Perkins School of*

5. Long, *Preaching the Literary Forms*, 87.

6. Blomberg, "Preaching the Parables," 33.

7. Lowry, *How to Preach a Parable*, 20–21.

8. Brice, *Parabolic Teaching of Christ*, 1.

9. Long, *Preaching and the Literary Forms*, 96–98.

10. Long, *Preaching and the Literary Forms*, 96–98.

Theology Journal 3, Fall 1983, by Richard Eslinger), and "Preaching on the Parable Genre" (in *Review and Expositor* 94, Spring 1997, by Peter Rhea Jones). All of these materials and more assisted me in the writing of this book and will be cited along the way.

I chose to use Long's book *Preaching the Literary Forms of the Bible* for two reasons. First, Long examines the parables as a biblical form that at first appears "preacher friendly," but "as soon as we reach out to grasp a parable's seemingly obvious truth, a trapdoor opens and fall through to a deeper and unexpected level of understanding."[11] That tension and challenge is intriguing to me and Long expresses it very effectively. As a homiletician, the challenge of preaching the parables of Jesus becomes a challenge I am willing and eager to accept.

The second reason for choosing Long's book is it was the focus of my doctor of ministry dissertation, "Thomas Long's Three Categories of Parables and Their Implications for Preaching," which I wrote for Harding University Graduate School of Religion in Memphis, Tennessee,[12] and was approved on April 28, 2006. The intensive research and writing of that document is an achievement of which I am very proud, and it formed a very firm foundation upon which to write this chapter in this book.

Long offers a homiletic that stresses literary form and rhetorical effect. The parables identified as "code" are read allegorically where "each important feature of a particular parable becomes a cipher for some unstated reality," understood only when the code is deciphered.[13] The code parable engages the readers in three ways: (1) they confirm and (2) they clarify what the readers already know and believe, and (3) they certify the readers as insiders.[14] Code parables "symbolize their nonliteral referent through the allegorical process . . . by matching each major aspect of the parable to a corresponding element in that deeper but hidden reality."[15] In other words, the code parable uses known symbols and terminology to emphasize a significant point found within the telling of the parable.

Parables identified as vessel act as simile and are "containers of concepts, general truths, or theological ideas."[16] Simile takes something the

---

11. Long, *Preaching and the Literary Forms*, 87.

12. It is now called Harding School of Theology.

13. Long, *Preaching and the Literary Forms*, 95.

14. Long, *Preaching and the Literary Forms*, 96–97.

15. Long, *Preaching and the Literary Forms*, 96.

16. Long, *Preaching and the Literary Forms*, 95.

reader does not understand and states it as something that is understood. A vessel parable embodies a single truth and is meant to be pedagogical, for "it teaches and illustrates that truth."[17] A vessel parable also employs certain "devices": (1) a series of episodes emphasizing the final episode and its meaning, (2) the language of comparison and contrast, asking how something can be and allowing the reader to say, "Aha, I see," and (3) the use of core truths as formulas that underline central ideas such as "the first will be last."[18]

In the category of parables as "objects of art," Long stresses the parables "that employ the dynamics of metaphor."[19] An object of art parable does not express what the audience already knows or what they can learn about the kingdom of God. Instead, the audience can expect to be drawn into the parable and experience the claim the parable is making about the kingdom.[20] The parable is not just about symbolism but has the desire to shock the reader, so to encourage a reaction.

Due to the large number of parables, I will examine only three examples. First, the parables of the hidden treasure and the pearl (Matt 13:44–46) can be simile, so then vessel because the kingdom is expressed in terms more familiar to the reader/listener. The parables can also be "objects of art," or metaphors, because they share the plot of finding, selling, and buying, drawing the reader into the world of the parable.[21]

Second, the parable of the good Samaritan (Luke 10:30–36) can be identified as vessel because the "end stress"[22] of the parable is relieved when the readers learn that the true neighbor is not the priest or Levite, but the Samaritan. The parable can also be viewed as "object of art" since it allows the reader to take on the identity of the priest, Levite, Samaritan, or the victim. So engaged, the reader is led to make a response to the parable.[23]

Third, the parable of the sower (Mark 4:1–9; Luke 8:4–8) can be identified as "code," for Mark 4:13–20 offers an allegorical explanation

---

17. Long, *Preaching and the Literary Forms*, 97.

18. Long, *Preaching and the Literary Forms*, 99–100.

19. Long, *Preaching and the Literary Forms*, 97.

20. Long, *Preaching and the Literary Forms*, 97.

21. Long, *Preaching and the Literary Forms*, 103–5. Long specifically mentions the parables of the hidden treasure and the pearl as examples of vessel and object.

22. Long uses this phrase to describe a rhetorical effect of the vessel parable; Long, *Preaching and the Literary Forms*, 99.

23. Long, *Preaching and the Literary Forms*, 99–100. Once again, Long offers the parable of the good Samaritan as an example of both vessel and object of art.

of the parable.[24] Yet, the parable can also be seen as an example of vessel because it contains the assurance of the great power of the word of God to be effective in spite of numerous obstacles.[25]

It is not adequate simply to define a parable as "an earthly story with a heavenly meaning."[26] The parable becomes, theologically, a vehicle of encounter with Jesus, revealing his view of life in the kingdom of God. The function of the parable is to illuminate some spiritual truth. The parable draws the listener/reader into it as a participant in its unfolding story and revealed truth. This participation is not merely experiential, but scripturally dynamic as the listener discovers the message Jesus intended.

Gail O'Day offers insight into this dynamic as she writes of the "conversation" between the text and the preacher.[27] Her method emphasizes the discovery of the three "voices" of the text: historical-critical exegesis, literary criticism, and "biblical preaching that focuses on the future of the biblical text and the world in front of the text."[28] The focus is preaching that invites the listener into the world of the text, revealing the theological and pastoral intent of the text.[29]

As a part of the "conversation" O'Day mentions the listener is active in the interpretation of the parable. Yet, its message must remain true to the gospel principles of Jesus Christ. The freshness of the parable must also be retained. Sidney Greidanus believes a key concern is that preachers must see the text as kerygma, proclamation, address, and the relevant word of God. He insists that relevant preaching allows the text to "address people today just as explicitly and concretely as it did in biblical times."[30]

Proper exegesis seeks the intent of the text; what did Jesus have in mind when he preached the parables? An examination of the parables

---

24. Jesus explains that, first, the seed sown on the path are people who hear the word, but Satan takes it away from them. Second, the seed sown among the rocks are those who hear the word with joy but lose their conviction. Third, the seed sown among thorns are those who allow the world to choke off spiritual fruit. Finally, the seed sown on good soil are those who hear the word and bear much fruit.

25. Long, *Preaching and the Literary Forms*, 98. Long also mentions the parable of the marriage feast (Matt 22:1–14) as an example of code.

26. I am uncertain as to the origin of this definition of the parables, but I have heard it used numerous times throughout the years.

27. O'Day, "Bible and Sermon," 69.

28. O'Day, "Bible and Sermon," 72.

29. O'Day, "Bible and Sermon," 75, 77–78.

30. Sidney Greidanus, *Modern Preacher*, 158–59.

of Jesus reveals that for the most part he told some of them to instruct or explain some aspect of Scripture. Other parables revealed the secrets of the kingdom. Sometimes the parables were understood well enough, while at other times the parable was not immediately understood, so the audience requested Jesus to explain the meaning. Stein writes that Jesus sometimes used parables to disarm all or part of an audience given to hostility or hardness of heart.

In Mark's gospel Jesus seems to indicate that he told parables to conceal information. In 4:10–12 Jesus said that the secrets of the kingdom of God had been given to the apostles, but to those "on the outside everything is said in parables." In this way they would see but never perceive and hear but never understand, "otherwise they might turn and be forgiven." How is this passage to be interpreted? Perhaps Jesus does not refer to the disciples versus the multitudes, but to those who understand versus those who do not. Perhaps Jesus revealed the kingdom's secrets only to his disciples but concealed such information from his antagonists. While the meaning of Jesus' explanation in Mark four is debated, it is clear that his parables were told to fulfill a purpose intended for those who would benefit the most by their message of the kingdom of God.

The parables of Jesus have a theological value and it is the purpose of this chapter to examine their theological value as the parables are preached. More specifically, I will examine the theological value of preaching the parables according to the three categories of the parables as proposed by Thomas Long. In addition, special attention will be given to how preaching the parables emerge in the nature of a theology of encounter.

Jesus brought his message into the world and that message was illustrated, in part, through the preaching of his parables. The parables of Jesus occupy a substantial portion of the Gospels and so are significant to the gospel itself. Frank Thielman comments, "If you open the New Testament somewhere toward the front and begin reading, chances are good that you will find yourself reading a parable. Something like thirty-five percent of Jesus' teaching as it is preserved in the gospels takes the form of parables."[31] There is a message to be learned in the parables and that message becomes central to grasping the theological value of the parables of Jesus that rests within that message.

The parables of Jesus offer a way to view a theology of the kingdom of God through an examination of the text. Within the parables of

31. Thielman, "Preaching the Parables," 27.

Jesus the identification of the "kingdom" becomes a metaphor for God's power manifested in the life and teaching of Jesus.[32] According to Craig Blomberg, theologically the parables identify the kingdom of God and in so doing they accomplish three things.[33] First, they teach about the sovereignty of God, for he is in command (e.g., Luke 17:7–10) and in control (e.g., Mark 4:3–9). Even though he is sovereign, God is patient with those who commit evil (e.g., Mark 12:1–9). His grace and mercy are greater than all expectations, for his judgment is not based on one's merit (Matt 20:1–16). So then, his justice is fair, meted out without bias (Matt 18:23–25; 21:28–32; Luke 13:6–9, 15; 16:19–31).

Second, the parables teach about God's people, who are identified as those who will deny themselves to seek "whole-hearted discipleship" (Luke 14:28–32; Matt 13:44–46).[34] God's people seek a life of spiritual stewardship (Matt 25:14–30). Being faithful stewards, they do not seek worldly possessions, but are in pursuit of the spiritual blessings of God (Luke 10:25–37; 12:13–21; 16:1–9; Matt 24:43; 35:30). As God's people they are given to prayer, which they offer boldly and without shame (Luke 11:5-8; 18:1-8).[35] They are concerned about the growth of the kingdom of God (e.g., Mark 4:1–34) and look forward to receiving the eternal rewards promised to them as the people of God (Matt 13:24–30; Luke 16:19–31).

Third, the parables teach about those who are not God's people. There are those who do not bear spiritual fruit and are spiritually uncommitted, even though they claim discipleship (Mark 12:1–9; Matt 21:28–32). Lives given to repentance and acts of mercy are what define true disciples, not a position in a religious organization (Luke 18:9–14). Those who are not God's people live in constant rebellion to his will (Luke 7:31–35; 14:16–24). They do not live as though they know the day of judgment is approaching (Matt 13:24–30; 18:23–35; 24:45; 25:30).

LONG'S CATEGORIES OF PARABLES

As the parables provide a means of understanding a theology of the kingdom of God, a method of interpreting those parables is needed. From that method of interpretation, a means of preaching the parables must also be

32. Donahue, *Gospel in Parable*, 378.

33. Blomberg, *Interpreting the Parables*, 293–95.

34. Blomberg, *Interpreting the Parables*, 293–95.

35. Blomberg, *Interpreting the Parables*, 294.

identified. The plethora of materials available to the student of parables and their myriad approaches for interpreting and preaching them has offered a wealth of information.

Thomas Long, in his book *Preaching the Literary Forms of the Bible* (1989), takes a literary approach to preaching the parables of Jesus.[36] Long's three categories of parables help us to understand how the kingdom of God and God's people are identified, and that assists in addressing the parables homiletically as well. Where Blomberg describes the nature of the kingdom,[37] Long offers the methodology by which the kingdom is seen displayed through the proclamation of the message contained therein.

The Category of Code

In Long's first category there are the parables identified as "code." Long places code in the realm of allegory, but Blomberg believes such a designation is misleading, preferring to "safeguard against overly elaborate and anachronistic allegorizing" by calling them "symbolic."[38] Norman Perrin, borrowing from Yeats, seeks to offer a contrast of allegory and symbolism, writing that symbolism says "things which could not be said so perfectly in any other way" and allegory and "things which could be said as well, or better, in another way."[39] Perrin's contrast helps us to see that allegory appears to fit the point of a code parable; that is, the thrust of the parable of code being discerned through an act of restatement.

Mike Graves, citing Bernard Brandon Scott, writes, "The symbol is what the parable refers to."[40] In other words, as code the parable reveals through symbol the message of the parable. Not only do parables reveal the kingdom of God through symbolism, but also in that symbolism there is evidence of theologies such as God's love and the person and nature of Christ. Graves continues, "The parabolic stories can communicate [truth] more powerfully than any propositional statement."[41]

In spite of any debate over proper terminology, Long holds fast to the parables of code being identified as allegorical. While Long concedes the

---

36. Long, *Preaching and the Literary Forms*, 11.

37. Blomberg, *Interpreting the Parables*, 290, 295–96.

38. Blomberg, *Interpreting the Parables*, 24.

39. Perrin, *Jesus and the Language*, 157.

40. Graves, *Sermon as Symphony*, 41.

41. Graves, *Sermon as Symphony*, 41.

role of the parables of code to be acts of symbolism, he does not abandon the designation of allegory in favor of the label of symbol.[42] Parables of code confirm what the reader already knows and believes, causing old information to be supported in new ways.[43] So then, the parables of code also clarify what is already known and believed, so nothing new is revealed, but what is known and believed is restated. In this way, in the parable of the wicked tenants or the wicked vinedressers (Matt 21:33–45; Mark 12:1–11; Luke 20:9–18) anyone who knows the relationship of God and Israel can see the same between a landlord and tenants.[44]

Long insists the concept of code can be seen in the parable of the sower (Mark 4; Luke 8). As code, the parable portrays or symbolizes the way the word of God is heard and accepted. The parable then is about the word of God, not agricultural concerns, and, says Robert L. Wilken, addresses this issue by describing each individual's responsibility of hearing, reception, and use of the word. Frank Stagg sees a doctrine of apostasy proclaimed in the parable and so then a theology of hearing or a theology of human potential and responsibility.[45]

Perhaps it would be better to say that the parable becomes an examination of the human responsibility to hear the word of God as it is preached, to ask, "What kind of soil am I?"[46] All of the word of God is good, so it is to be heard and accepted. The word of God is the focus of the parable of the sower. The word is preached and is able to yield a great harvest if only one will hear it.

The Category of Vessel

In Long's second category there are the parables identified as vessel, which he describes as simile. Parables that emerge as vessel or simile, according to Long, point to one aspect of the deeper reality they symbolize. "They are

---

42. Long, *Preaching and the Literary Forms*, 96. This view is derived from Long's discussion of the parables of code. In it he admits that the parables of code "symbolize their nonliteral referent through the allegorical process." By saying that, I would assume he sees these parables as allegorical and being allegorical they function in the realm of symbolism.

43. Long, *Preaching and the Literary Forms*, 96–97.

44. Long, *Preaching and the Literary Forms*, 97.

45. Wilken, "In Defense of Allegory," 199.

46. Hunter, "Interpreting the Parables," part 2, 172.

designed to embody a single truth," he writes.[47] So then, a vessel parable is pedagogical, for it illustrates a specific point through the use of comparison and contrast, such as the identity of the true neighbor and a Samaritan (Luke 10), the kingdom revealed as small, but great (Luke 13:18–21), and an unjust judge and a just God (Luke 18:2–8).

Long identifies the parable of the good Samaritan (Luke 10:25–37) as a vessel parable, so then an example of simile. Several themes from the parable have been proposed. Of course, the theme of compassion is obvious, for the Samaritan is revealed as the neighbor because of his compassion to the fallen man (Luke 10:33, 36). Peter Rhea Jones claims a theme of abandonment, citing the abuse and abandonment of the robbers, the abandonment of the "religionists," and the "compassionate overcoming of abandonment."[48] Brett Younger detects a theme of confrontation, for to preach something so unsettling, and so then confrontational, is to preach as Jesus did.

The themes of compassion, abandonment, and confrontation are creative approaches to the parable homiletically. First, building from the question of inheriting eternal life and, second, the identity of one's neighbor, the parable becomes an account of compassion: as are we, so was the victim; as Jesus Christ is, so was the Samaritan. We must seek a Christlike compassion toward all.

According to Lischer, a theology of preaching includes a rearticulation of the theology of the church by proclaiming the essence of kingdom, Christ, and salvation.[49] That being the case, the parable of the good Samaritan expresses the Christ, his kingdom, and his salvation through the abandonment of the victim, the compassion of the Samaritan, and the encouragement of Jesus to do likewise if one will inherit that kingdom (Luke 10:36–37).

All three parables under consideration in this chapter can be read as vessels or simile. As the Sower is code or allegory, in that it confirms and clarifies what the reader knows and believes, it is also vessel because it points to something deeper than just agricultural practices. It proclaims the truth about those who are fitted for the kingdom of heaven, those who long for a bountiful spiritual harvest.

In the parable of the pearl and the hidden treasure, which is considered as one parable for this dissertation, the fact that the kingdom is worth

---

47. Long, *Preaching and the Literary Forms*, 97.

48. Jones, "Preaching on the Parable Genre," 236–37.

49. Richard Lischer, *Theories of Preaching*, 2.

every effort to obtain it, to sell all and buy it, becomes its single truth. It is simile because the theological point is not about treasure or pearls, but about what comes only from Jesus Christ. To preach these parables as examples of vessel is to proclaim the power of Jesus to build his kingdom. The word of God, as described by seed sown, riches found, and a compassionate neighbor, comes alive through the message of the parables.

Category of Object of Art

Long's third category are the parables of "object of art" or metaphor. Stated simply, in a metaphor A is B and C is D. Examples would include "a heart of stone" or "the apple of my eye." These parables, being metaphorical in form, reveal something extraordinary, so the reader/listener is shocked.[50] Within an object of art parable there is a surprise element or a strange twist that leads the reader/listener to say, "I never imagined!"

Norman Perrin comments, "In a simile 'the less known is clarified by the better known,' but in a metaphor 'two discrete and not entirely comparable elements' are juxtaposed, and this juxtaposition 'produces an impact upon the imagination and induces a vision of that which cannot be conveyed by prosaic or discursive speech.'"[51] Put another way, as code (allegory) reveals what is known, an object of art reveals what is not known. In this way, the reader/listener is forced to make a judgment regarding what is revealed. That judgment emerges from the shock, the surprise that leads the reader/listener to come to grasp with what has been revealed.

In the examination of the parable of the good Samaritan as vessel or simile earlier it was noted that one of the themes that might emerge homiletically is confrontation. The same can be said with metaphor; in fact, it might be more so with metaphor. By its nature, the object of art parable confronts the reader/listener with the word of God and its shocking, surprising, and even paradoxical message.

Such a confrontation pushes the reader/listener to reflect theologically, an act that leads to belief. This is what preaching the parable genre does in general, claims C. Clifton Black, for by its very nature preaching is parabolic "because [it] is that jarring-but-exquisite clash of inescapable human need with the merciful power of God."[52] The confrontation, that

50. Long, *Preaching and the Literary Forms*, 97.
51. Perrin, *Jesus and the Language*, 135.
52. C. Clifton Black, "Four Stations en Route," 388.

which shocks and surprises and that which leads to making a judgment, points toward the kingdom and, so then, God.

A portion of a theology of preaching, as Lischer puts it, is "a theology,"[53] which he uses to indicate a reflection on God. Preaching the object of art parable must do just that. Since preaching must obtain its authority from the authority of the word itself, the parabolic object of art sermon must express the authority of the word to make its revelation of God and his kingdom in an extraordinary way.

A THEOLOGY OF ENCOUNTER AND PREACHING THE KINGDOM

The message of the parables of Jesus projects a theological view of the kingdom of God that emerges in their interpretation. Yet, their theology is rendered stagnant without a method of making a connection between the parable and the reader/listener. As noted earlier, Blomberg insists identifying the kingdom of God in the parables accomplishes three things: (1) they teach about the sovereignty of God, (2) they teach about God's people, and (3) they teach about those who are not God's people.[54] Blomberg's observations are well taken, but something more is needed.

Blomberg's theological view of the kingdom in the parables is rendered stagnant if those methods of identification do not make a connection to the people of God. Otherwise, they are little more than theologies on the pages of manuscripts targeted to the elite few. It is well and good to engage in textual interpretation, but until that interpretation is allowed to illuminate the message of the text and so lead to an encounter with the people of God, it remains little more than theological words. That is why Long's categories of the parables offer significant assistance in bringing the message of those parables off of the printed page and placing it into the lives of the readers/listeners. As I mentioned before, the parables invite the reader/listener into the world of the text where there is an encounter with its theological and pastoral intent.

Graves believes the parables are "open-ended," but that term should not be misunderstood. The open-ended nature of the parables does not leave its interpretation entirely with the reader/listener but makes the reader/listener part of its application. He writes:

53. Lischer, *Theories of Preaching*, 9.

54. Blomberg, *Interpreting the Parables*, 293–96.

> Jesus' parables are open-ended experiences that force listeners to make application to themselves. . . . It seems likely that Jesus' listeners, upon hearing the parable of the farmer who stumbled on buried treasure, might respond in two entirely different ways. Some might have exclaimed, "Oh, my God, I never imagined." Others, however, might have gone home thinking, "Well, I never really thought about finding treasure out in my field." Parables are for those who have ears.[55]

What the parable communicates is two-dimensional: the secular and religious, our world and God's world. As the parable unfolds, the reader/listener comes in contact with Jesus and the moral truth of life within the kingdom of God. As one hears or reads the parable, he is drawn into it as a participant, making the story, told by Jesus in his own context, the reader/listener's story as well. That encounter allows the parable to be "open-ended," a connection between the text, its story, and those who have ears to hear it.

The nature of encounter fits nicely within Long's categories of parables. By their very nature, parables of code or allegory allow the reader/listener to encounter the text because the parable reveals what is already known and believed. In this way, the reader/listener already has a connection with the parable, for nothing new is revealed. He enters the story as an insider who awaits the telling of what is known in a new way.

In the parable of the sower, for example, the reader/listener is aware of the act of planting seed and harvest and how the seed can symbolize the word as it is preached. Instead of something obscure, requiring further information for a connection to be made, the parable emerges from something the reader/listener understands. The encounter is then extended into the responsibility for the message of the parable to be heard.

In the parables of vessel or simile, an encounter is made through the pedagogical nature of the parable. What is unknown or obscure becomes known through the instructional function of the vessel parable. For instance, the parable of the good Samaritan is founded upon the question, "Teacher, what shall I do to inherit eternal life?" (Luke 10:25). While the reader believes he knows the answer to the question, the parable unfolds to reveal an answer unknown before. The reader/listener is instructed in a new way. The reader/listener makes an encounter with the kingdom of God by seeing it in a way not realized before.

55. Graves, *Sermon as Symphony*, 44.

Finally, an encounter is made in the parables of object of art or metaphor. The encounter occurs when the reader/listener realizes what was expected is the opposite of what actually occurs (for example, the priest and Levite do not aid the victim). What they might have done in similar circumstances is the same as the Samaritan and not those who would be expected to help. Such an encounter forces the reader/listener to reflect on the meaning of what is so shocking and surprising. As they contemplate the parable and its unexpected twists and turns, the act of reflection on what has occurred leads to a contemplation of the personal expectations of the reader/listener, and that leads to belief.

We can appreciate Mark Thomsen's observations on the nature of encounter within the parables: "We encounter the Lord of the kingdom who is present and speaks through the parables. Preaching can never ignore that the content of Jesus' message is fused with its original parabolic form."[56] Notice that Thomsen rightfully connects the process of encounter with the task of preaching.

It is in this way the parable becomes scripturally dynamic, for the message of Jesus is discovered and proclaimed, and that message expresses the truth of Jesus Christ in a dynamic way, making the old story a new story. A sense of freshness is retained, and the parable becomes consistently viable and obtainable each time it is read and preached.

So then, preaching the parables should invite the reader/listener into the world of the text, seeking to grasp its theological and pastoral intent. Preaching the parables must embrace the encounter of the text with the reader/listener and the truth that is revealed in that encounter. Hunter comments, "But if the parable is meant to quicken understanding, it requires that the hearer be in some kind of spiritual rapport with its teller, if he is to divine the heavenly truth behind the earthly story."[57] The kingdom is revealed and the reader/listener is brought into the world of the parable as Jesus expresses it. That encounter can be an essential part of preaching.

Preaching the parables is effective when it reflects the literary form of that parable. For example, Donahue speaks of the surprise element or strange twist,[58] such as in the parable of the good Samaritan. It is not the priest or the Levite, but the Samaritan, the perceived enemy and false worshiper, who is the neighbor.

56. Thomsen, "Parabolic Theology," 202.

57. Hunter, "Interpreting the Parables," part 1, 74.

58. Donahue, "Jesus as the Parable," 380.

The strange twist in the parable occurs in the final episode where vital information is given that thrusts the focus of the parable forward. Graves writes that this sort of parable makes use of "end stress," for "the identity of the man (a Samaritan) who stopped to help is only revealed well into Jesus' story." Preaching can take this "twist" or "end stress" and use it to proclaim the message of the parable to the audience.

How, then, does the nature of encounter inform the task of preaching the parables? When preaching a parable, the preacher must keep its kingdom message in mind, as well as the interaction of the text and audience that arises as the parable is read or proclaimed. The parable is more than a story and through its parabolic form it becomes the vehicle of a scriptural message, and that message must be understood and accepted. A theology of human potential and responsibility arises in the very purpose and nature of parables. Frank Stagg points out key words in the parables such as *akouete* ("to hear; to understand") in, for example, Mark's account of the parable of the sower that illustrate the audience's responsibility in encountering the parables.[59]

So, what does this mean? How is the parable to be preached? The intent of the parable, its message, must be ascertained and that message must then be proclaimed. Preaching the parables does not encompass a mere retelling of the story. Jesus had a specific reason for presenting the parable and that must be respected in its interpretation and presentation. Put simply, the central message of the parable is the kingdom of God and the message of the kingdom Jesus wanted his audience to see. That message is illuminated by observing how the parable may be read: as code (allegory), vessel (simile), or object of art (metaphor). Through presenting what is known but in a new way (code), through instructing the reader/listener (vessel), or through shock and surprise (object of art), preaching the parables is meant to illuminate the parable's scriptural intent.

The parable carries within it a scriptural dynamic that resonates with the intentions of Jesus and his message of the kingdom. That dynamic is allowed to emerge in the interactive encounter of the audience with the parable. The reader/listener is drawn into the world of the parable and reacts to what the parable reveals. Yet, the end result is not something found only in a personal encounter, but in theological reflection that illuminates the central moral truth Jesus intended. In this way, the reader/listener becomes a participant in the revelation of that moral truth.

59. Stagg, "Luke's Theological Use of Parables," 221.

Preaching a parable must respect this scriptural and theological dynamic. The sermon becomes the way the hearer encounters the intended message, and that message encompasses the truth to be known.

HOW THE PARABLES MIGHT BE BIBLICALLY PREACHED

Thomas Long insists that biblical preaching can be observed through the various literary forms found in the biblical text: psalms, proverbs, narratives, epistles, and parables. The last of these is the subject of this study. In his book, *Preaching the Literary Forms of the Bible* (1989), Long notes the two arenas in which the text is both exegetically and hermeneutically observed: in the "academy" and in the act of preaching.[60] "The best scholarship," he writes, "I am convinced, is done by those who work while hearing the sound of the preacher, concerned about next Sunday's sermon, knocking on the study door."[61]

One of the ways these two worlds have been connected is by textual interpretation through literary and rhetorical methods and, if it is completely and effectively done, it must culminate in the act of proclaiming the message of the text.

In chapter 2 the issue of a theology of preaching the parables of Jesus was addressed. In that investigation, it was noted that in preaching the parables two theologies arise: a theology of the kingdom and a theology of encounter, with considerations of the connection made between the text and the reader/listener.

How does a sermon look if it proclaims a parable as code (allegory), vessel (simile), and object of art (metaphor) according to Long? How would a sermon differ if it addressed the same parable, but in two of the three literary ways Long proposes? In a similar thought, how would two parables compare and contrast if observed through the same literary lens?

The purpose of this chapter is to examine how the parable of the hidden treasure and the pearl (Matt 13:44–46) can be preached as vessel and object of art, how the parable of the good Samaritan (Luke 10:30–37) can be preached as vessel and object of art, and how the parable of the sower (Mark 4:1–9, 13–20; Luke 8:4–8) can be preached as code and vessel. After an exposition of the text of each parable, two full-text sermons

60. Long, *Preaching and the Literary Forms*, 7.

61. Long, *Preaching and the Literary Forms*, 7–8.

will be presented, as they will be delivered to the Johnson congregation, representing the specific literary forms mentioned above. Doing this, the way the literary form shapes the sermon should become evident and the parabolic categories of Long and their implications for preaching will be tested for their merit.

The Parable of the Hidden Treasure and the Pearl (Matt 13:44–46)

The hidden treasure and the pearl are two paradigmatic parables contained in a collection of several in Matt 13. By "paradigmatic" I mean they follow a specific pattern or paradigm, one which both share. The parable of the sower, which is also a part of this book, is another example of a paradigmatic parable. The two parables function as a unit that, as Matthean scholarship has long observed, "forms a turning point in the flow of the Gospel."[62]

Long calls these parables "advent-reversal-action" parables, for in the unexpected finding of treasure, the man receives something unexpectedly great.[63] In the same way, the merchant in his purposeful search for pearls finds one that is better than expected. In both cases, something to be treasured is found. This is the nature of "advent-reversal-action," those moments in life that result in unexpected discovery.

Long does not indicate how the parables function as "advent-reversal-action" parables, but Crossan does:

> The future [the man] had presumably planned and projected for himself is totally invalidated by the *advent* of the Treasure that opens up new world and unforeseen possibilities. In the force of this advent, he willingly *reverses* his entire past. . . . It gives him a new world of life and *action* he did not have before, and he could not have programmed for himself.[64]

The "advent-reversal-action" scheme of the parables becomes a description of how the man's world forever changes. It also describes the movement of the parables from discovery to decision to action as the story unfolds, something that is not to be lost in the telling.

---

62. Long, *Preaching and the Literary Forms*, 103.

63. Long, *Preaching and the Literary Forms*, 105.

64. Crossan, *In Parables*, 34.

The story of the parables is rather simple. The kingdom of heaven is compared, first, to treasure hidden in a field. A man accidentally finds it and thinking quickly, reburies the treasure, sells all he possesses, and uses the money to buy the land where the treasure is hidden. Second, the kingdom is compared to a merchant who finds a pearl of great value among many others. He also sells all he possesses and purchases the pearl.

The parables are comparable in their telling: (1) something valuable that is hidden, whether it is treasure hidden in a field or a pearl hidden among other pearls; (2) the finding of what has been hidden or searched for; (3) the selling of personal possessions; (4) the purchasing of what is more valuable.

Comparison and contrast are a factor of a vessel parable, which is one way this study observes the parables of the treasure and the pearl. Of course, comparisons and contrasts of the two men are made regarding their identity. Speaking of the first parable, Bernard Scott insists, "Because the parable begins with hidden treasure, we know nothing about the one who will find it."[65]

Such a view does not stop some from making assumptions. Michael Green sees a contrast of the two men in these parables: the man who finds the treasure is poor and the man who finds the pearl is rich.[66] C. H. Dodd agrees that it is an impoverished man who stumbles upon the treasure.[67] Robert Stein, however, offers something more concrete by taking notice of the *sokher*, the day laborer who worked the fields of another in ancient Palestine.[68] He indicates that being a *sokher* places the man in the field so that he might find the treasure. Yet, being a paid employee of another, the land does not belong to him, so he purchases it to gain ownership of the treasure he has found. Even though this may be the case, it is not certain and may assume more than what the parable reveals.

Another contrast is the subtle change from accidentally finding something hidden to purposefully searching for something hidden among others like it. Each man finds something wonderful, but each does so in a different way.

Historically, the parables would make sense to the contemporary audience. Treasure was often buried during times of distress such as war

---

65. Scott, *Hear Then the Parable*, 395.

66. Green, *Message of Matthew*, 159.

67. Dodd, *Parables of the Kingdom*, 84.

68. Stein, *Introduction to the Parables*, 100.

and changes in rulers, such as in the account of the fall of Jerusalem by Josephus and how the Romans found much of the city's wealth which the inhabitants had stored underground.[69] Circumstances sometimes caused the treasure to be forgotten and then found at a later date by someone else. Likewise, the ancient world knew well the merchant in search of excellent wares. Unlike the modern-day obsession with gold, the pearl was highly prized in the ancient world, so it is acceptable that the merchant would be looking for pearls.

What is implied in these two parables is the kingdom of heaven, indicated by the introductory phrase "the kingdom of heaven is like" found in both. What is revealed about the kingdom, however? Green believes the parables indicate the kingdom is found in many ways: some by accident and others after "a long and patient search."[70] Blomberg does not necessarily disagree but writes that it is not only the search that is the point, but the finding of something so worthwhile; that the kingdom is of such tremendous value.[71]

D. A. Carson expands upon Blomberg by emphasizing "the supreme importance of the kingdom" in the parables.[72] To Carson, the kingdom in the parables is something far beyond what was sold or given up. Carson continues, "The kingdom of heaven is worth infinitely more than the cost of discipleship, and those who know where the treasure lies joyfully abandon everything else to secure it."[73] Green echoes this conclusion, writing, "It is immensely worthwhile, however we come on it. It is treasure. It is a beautiful pearl. It is worth any sacrifice."[74]

The parables illuminate the kingdom in its grandest sense, something worth more than anything one might possess; though the day laborer would sell all he has, his inheritance of the kingdom offers spiritual wealth beyond any worldly treasure or a pearl at any price. Those who seek the kingdom do well, regardless of the effort and expenditure.

---

69. Scott (*Hear Then the Parable*, 395) cites Josephus, *Jewish War*, 7.5.2.

70. Green, *Message of Matthew*, 160.

71. Blomberg, *Interpreting the Parables*, 279.

72. Carson, *Expositor's Bible Commentary*, 328.

73. Carson, *Expositor's Bible Commentary*, 328.

74. Green, *Message of Matthew*, 160.

Preaching the Parable of the Hidden Treasure and the Pearl of Great Value as Vessel

What would a sermon about the parables of the hidden treasure and the pearl look like if they were preached as a vessel or simile? The presence of this literary form is rather obvious, for each parable is formed from the statement "the kingdom of heaven is like" (Matt 13:44, 45), the "is like" being a standard indicator of vessel. The strength of the vessel parable is its ability to instruct, what Long describes as, "Aha, I see!"[75]

The two parables under consideration emerge as vessel because they reveal a specific point not understood before. There is an unknown element in the vessel parable and that element must be revealed for the truth to be known. To merely say something "is like" something else is too broad, so when one reads or hears a vessel parable the contrast of the "is like" statement must be revealed. The message of the parable is seen in that one point of contrast, for the vessel connects the known and the unknown at that one point.[76]

The reader might wonder how the kingdom of God can be comparable to finding hidden treasure or a costly pearl and he would do well to wonder, for the comparison is unusual. The vessel sermon intends to illuminate the kingdom of God in a new way, in this case as something to be searched for and found. The acts of searching and finding become the focus of the vessel sermon.

A vessel sermon arising from both of these parables will instruct the listener to embrace a certain truth about the kingdom of God. In the case of the sermon below, it is the fact that the kingdom of God is worth whatever it takes to obtain it, illuminated not only through the imagery of the parables themselves, but through other New Testament examples as well.

The parables, when preached as vessel, might look like the following.

"Look What I Have Found"

I have sometimes wondered about those who survey the beaches and fields of our country and even throughout the world with metal detectors. Day after day they go in search of rings, coins, or other metal objects, always

75. Long, *Preaching and the Literary Forms*, 97.

76. Long, *Preaching and the Literary Forms*, 97.

harboring in the backs of their minds the dream of finding something valuable, some sort of treasure.

Imagine finding a valuable piece of jewelry, such as a ring encrusted with diamonds and other precious stones. There is no engraving and no sort of identifying marks, just someone's very expensive ring lying on the ground. What would you do? Who would you contact? Do you follow the rule of "finders keepers, losers weepers"[77] or do you contact the police to report what you have found? Would you have to contact anyone at all? If there is a price to pay to keep it, what price are you willing to pay for treasure? How much would be too much?

Matthew records a parable of Jesus about someone who had just such an experience. The parable is very short, just one verse, and reads as follows from the NIV: "The kingdom of heaven is like treasure hidden in a field. When a man found it, he hid it again. And then in his joy went and sold all he had and bought that field" (Matt 13:44).

Did this man also wonder what he should do and whom he should contact? The parable does not indicate any sort of dilemma, only the desire to obtain what he had found. Dodd wonders if the man was "a fool to impoverish himself for the sake of buying the field."[78] Perhaps, but Dodd admits that the point is bigger than the loss or gain of money, but "the value of the property," which of course addresses more than just possessions.

I mentioned above the issue of "finders keepers, losers weepers" and how those who make unexpected discoveries face such a dilemma. The man in the parable, however, did not approach the experience with a "finders keepers, loser's weepers" mentality, but sought to purchase the land where the treasure had been found.

This man's world of "past-present-future" had been "rudely but happily shattered" by his discovery and his decision to purchase the land where the treasure was found.[79] In his mind, in order for him to obtain the treasure he had found he would first have to possess the land that contained it. From now on, nothing could be the same.

Imagine also going in search of something very special, perhaps something collectable such as an antique table. You search the antique

---

77. Brandon Scott believes so, insisting that "finder's keepers, loser's weepers" describes the discovery of treasure that rests in a field the finder does not yet own. In fact, the chapter that discusses this parable is even entitled, "Finder's Keepers" (*Hear Then the Parable*, 389).

78. Dodd, *Parables of the Kingdom*, 85.

79. Crossan, *In Parables*, 34.

stores throughout the county and find piece after piece at a variety of prices, all of them expensive. Finally, you stop at a small shop along the road and begin to look around. There are a wide variety of tables and all of them are little more than dust-covered junk. Then you see it, a table sitting in a corner serving as a place for several small items to be displayed. On closer examination, you realize the beauty and craftsmanship of this table and its worth far beyond anything else you have seen in any other shop. What would you do with such a find? How would you feel? What would you be willing to give up in order to obtain such a rare and valuable antique table for your home?

Jesus follows up his parable of the hidden treasure with a second parable of a merchant who had an experience similar to that of the scenario above. It is recorded as follows: "Again, the kingdom of heaven is like a merchant looking for fine pearls. When he found one of great value, he went away and sold everything he had and bought it" (Matt 13:45–46).

These parables insist that the kingdom of heaven is like finding treasure hidden in a field and the discovery of a pearl of great value, but what does that mean? In the parable of the hidden treasure, Crossan has noticed "three different strands within this advent: hiddenness and mystery ('hidden' in Matt. 13:44a), gift and surprise ('found' in 13:44b), discovery and joy ('joy' in 13:44c)."[80] These "strands" form a series of experiences and emotions that are expressed in both the man and in the reader/listener who encounters the parables.

Notice that Jesus describes the hidden treasure in a general way; instead of just gold or silver, this treasure is every form of precious metals and stones. It is just a treasure and not a specific type of treasure. In this way, the focus is not the treasure itself, but what that treasure represents in the parable. Jesus describes the kingdom of heaven as something truly worthy in all of its righteousness, peace, hope, and promises.

The kingdom is described elsewhere as something worthy of our possession. Consider Jesus' warning against possessions: food, drink, and clothing (Matt 6:25-34). Jesus insists that our heavenly Father knows that we need such things, so we should first seek the kingdom of God and his righteousness, and all of these other things will be given to us. In other words, the kingdom is worth more than all of our earthly possessions. So, then the kingdom of heaven is worthy of our discovery, whether that

---

80. Crossan, *In Parables*, 38.

discovery is made incidentally, as in the case of the treasure in the field, or as the result of a search for it, as in the case of the pearl.

The apostle Paul, for example, discovered the kingdom of heaven through some disconnected incident. Before his calling as an evangelist and apostle of the Lord, Saul (later called Paul) was pursuing things against the kingdom (Acts 9). As a persecutor of Christianity, his intentions were anything but kingdom centered. Yet, Jesus had other plans for him and, upon Saul's approach to the city of Damascus, confronted him with a detour in his life's journey. Asking Saul why he sought to persecute the Lord, Jesus instructed him to go on into the city and receive further instructions. Those instructions would begin the next chapter in the life of this persecutor turned apostle of the Lord.

It is significant that Luke would summarize the final portion of Paul's life in this world as bold and unhindered proclamation of the kingdom of God and the Lord Jesus (Acts 28:31). Crossan sees a connection with what he calls the "Damascus-Arabia-Jerusalem" conversion experience of Paul (Gal 1:15–18) and the "advent-reversal-action" scheme mentioned earlier.[81] Paul had stumbled upon the treasure of the kingdom on the road approaching Damascus. He had been confronted with a marvelous discovery, one he could not ignore when he realized what he had found.

Just as the man in the first parable, Paul had to possess the treasure that had been hidden from eyes blinded to everything else but the persecution of the church. It literally took the blindness of his eyes to make him see what lay at his feet, the treasure of the kingdom of heaven.

What of the analogy of the kingdom of heaven being like the discovery of a pearl of great value? Unlike Saul, who stumbled upon the kingdom when he was not looking for it, how can one miss such a wonderful discovery when he is in search of it? Surely if I am searching for something as grand and glorious as the kingdom of heaven it will rise up before me for me to unmistakably identify in vivid clarity.

Nicodemus (John 3:1–21) was a teacher of the Jewish law. He approached Jesus one night proclaiming that he and some others, Joseph of Arimathea perhaps, knew Jesus to be from God; this was evident from the many miraculous signs they had seen Jesus perform. Yet, Jesus saw more in Nicodemus's purpose perhaps, for he said, "I tell you the truth, no one can see the kingdom of God unless he is born again" (John 3:3). When Nicodemus failed to understand what Jesus was saying, the Lord instructed

81. Crossan, *In Parables*, 34.

him on three things: (1) being born again spiritually, (2) the extent of God's love for the world, and (3) the light that had been sent into the world.

Nicodemus had come in search of something, probably verification of his perceived justification, which he felt was evidenced by his function as one of Israel's teachers and his knowledge of the divine origin of Jesus' ministry. What he received, however, was a priceless gift: instruction from the Lord himself regarding his incarnation, mission, and coming sacrifice for the salvation of the world. To use the imagery of the parable, Nicodemus felt he already possessed a precious pearl but discovered another of unsurpassed beauty and value: the Son of God.

Students at the University of Arkansas traveled to a local site in search of ammonoid fossils, a spiral-shelled cephalopod.[82] A couple of students were digging into the soft soil near a drainage ditch searching for fossils between a few inches to three feet long. One of them, a freshman, noticed a bulge in the layer of shale below the surface and alerted her professor, and soon the two of them we hard at work, excavating the spot for its hidden treasures.

After a while, the work was finished, and their discovery was fully exposed. Instead of a fossil of a few inches in length, one commonly found in the state of Arkansas, they had uncovered a nine-foot nautiloid, a squid-like, straight-shelled cephalopod. It is the largest fossil of its kind ever found in the world. They were searching for something rather common but found something extraordinary.

For what do you or I search? What do we consider to be treasure worth searching for and finding? Perhaps the irony of the two parables is that for many people either experience would be immensely satisfying. Some dream of finding the rare book, the valuable jewel, or the historical artifact that would bring them fame and fortune. Their satisfaction does not come in the search that results in a valuable discovery, but in the discovery itself that comes without any effort to search. Jesus, however, in telling of such an experience actually has something much greater in mind: finding the immensity of the kingdom of heaven.

Paul knew this experience quite well. He told the Christians in Philippi that he understood the pursuits of worldly gain—what he calls "confidence in the flesh" (Phil 3:4). You see he had a great deal to boast of in this world, what with his lineage, upbringing, education, and sense of integrity. He insisted, however, whatever was profitable in this world he

82. Marberry, "Students Make Big Discovery."

considered a loss for Christ's sake when compared to knowing Jesus Christ as Lord, "for whose sake I have lost all things" (3:8). To him, these things were nothing but "rubbish," for his only purpose was to "gain Christ and be found in him" (3:9). So, what, then, was his purpose? He states it clearly: "that I may know him and the power of his resurrection, and may share his sufferings, becoming like him in his death, that by any means possible I may attain the resurrection of the dead" (3:10-11).

The kingdom of heaven is worth any price and any sacrifice, for there is nothing to surpass it. It is a treasure discovered unexpectedly and it is the greatest of pearls discovered when one searches for it. Each and every one can possess it if they search for it. The kingdom of heaven is worth every effort to obtain it. The result is not wealth in this world, but salvation in the kingdom of heaven. "Look what I have found," shouts the finder of spiritual treasure. "It is the kingdom of heaven and it is mine!"

Preaching the Parable of the Hidden Treasure and the Pearl of Great Value as Object of Art

How would this parable look when preached in the literary form of metaphor, or in Long's category of "object of art"? Long distinguishes these parables being viewed as vessel and object of art. He acknowledges that they can be seen as vessel, due in part to the phrase "the kingdom of heaven is like" that begins each parable. In this way, "the reader is led toward reading [the parable of the hidden treasure] as a vessel."[83]

It is reading the two parables together, Long insists, that leads the reader/listener to examine them again. This is not because the vessel reading of the parable of the treasure is incorrect, but because the second parable (the pearl) is to be read with the treasure parable.

After reading the second parable, it is determined that "the parables are matched not because they are vessels which contain the same idea but because they are brief narratives which share the same essential plot. . . . It is the plots which draw the readers into the world of the two parables."[84] Long insists the parables are to be read as objects of art,[85] but this study examines the parables as both since they evidence the elements of vessel as well as object of art.

83. Long, *Preaching and the Literary Forms*, 104.
84. Long, *Preaching and the Literary Forms*, 105.
85. Long, *Preaching and the Literary Forms*, 100.

Preaching the parable as object of art means that the sermon seeks to do what an object of art does, that is, draw the reader/listener into the world the parable has formed. This is done when the reader/listener is able to identify with one of the characters through the images within the parable. This is done because the reader/listener is drawn into the parable and its claims. The word "drawn" is indicative of the atmosphere of an object of art parable. Long quotes Norman Perrin in saying the object of art parable "produces shock to the imagination . . . which induces a new vision of world."[86] Since object of art utilizes plot, the sermon must take the plot formed within the parable and allow it to connect with those who will participate in its telling.

To repeat Long's claim, preaching the object of art parable is not to try and explain anything, as in a vessel sermon, but to reveal the world of the kingdom.[87] In this way the reader/listener is not on the outside looking in, but on the inside as a participant. This is because the object of art parable is presented in an open-ended way. In other words, the reader/listener is told enough information to allow him or her to make the experience of a character in the parable one's own.[88] The object of art parable is preached with no more intention to explain its content than one would need to explain a joke. The listener "simply 'gets it,' because one understands the punch line."[89]

Long insists that the parables of the hidden treasure and the pearl are seen best as objects of art; in fact, "they demand to be read as objects of art."[90] While I do not agree with his assessment that the parables "are clearly not vessels,"[91] I do agree that the parables are best read as objects of art because they carry the dynamics of metaphor: the unfolding of plot, the emergence of the unexpected, and the placement of the reader into the world of the story.

---

86. Long, *Preaching and the Literary Forms*, 97. Perrin, *Jesus and the Language*, 202.

87. Long, *Preaching and the Literary Forms*, 105.

88. Long, *Preaching and the Literary Forms*, 100–101.

89. Blomberg, "Preaching the Parables," 21–22.

90. Long, *Preaching and the Literary Forms*, 105.

91. Long, *Preaching and the Literary Forms*, 105. Long claims that in reading the hidden treasure it appears the parable is to be identified as vessel. When the pearl is read, however, the two parables come to be reconsidered not as vessels, but as objects of art. I believe the parables can be read as vessels or simile because they fit the literary form of simile.

A sermon about the parables of the hidden treasure and the pearl, when preached as object of art, might look like the following.

"What Are We Willing to Sell?"

In May 1844 the renowned biblical scholar Constantin Tischendorf arrived at the Monastery of St. Catherine on Mount Sinai and a few days later, while working in the library, noticed a large basket filled with manuscripts fragments.[92] Told they were rubbish, he was granted permission to examine them, finding 129 leaves in Greek that he saw to be sections of the Old Testament. He judged them to be no later than the fourth century, making them older than anything he had ever seen. His enthusiasm caused the librarian, a man named Cyril, to become suspicious and allowed Tischendorf to keep only 43 of the 129 leaves.[93]

Tischendorf assumed that somewhere in the monastery a large cache of manuscripts similar to those he had found was surely hidden. Returning in 1853 and then again in 1859, Tischendorf was shown "a bulky kind of volume, wrapped in a red cloth." The monk had searched the monastery and soon found much more of the Old Testament and the entire New Testament, in addition to the Epistle of Barnabas and the early portion of the *Shepherd of Hermas*.[94] What had begun as a chance discovery in a trash can turned out to be the finding of one the most significant manuscripts in existence. Tischendorf had found the Codex Sinaiticus, the fourth-century manuscript of the Bible, now residing in the British Museum in London.

Another, more familiar story of a great discovery features the work of one Howard Carter, an Egyptologist in the early twentieth century. Searching the Valley of the Kings in Egypt, Carter came upon a promising spot. Through proper archaeological technique, Carter eventually discovered a staircase and at the bottom of the staircase he found a door. That door led into a small chamber where Carter cut a small hole in the far wall. An ancient and musty smell wafted through to Carter and his associates. Lighting a candle, Carter peered into another chamber on the other side of the wall. When asked what he saw, he replied, "Wonderful things!" Howard Carter had found the tomb of Tutankhamun, King Tut.

92. Skeat, "Last Chapter," 313.

93. Skeat, "Last Chapter," 314.

94. Skeat, "Last Chapter," 314.

We enjoy reading about those who find interesting, important, and valuable things, especially if the discovery is accidental or if the find is greater than anticipated. The thrill of vicarious discovery fills us with a certain sense of adventure and satisfaction. We wonder what it would be like to do as they have done, to make such a discovery. All of a sudden, we are Indiana Jones finding the lost ark of the covenant or Lewis and Clark looking at the Rocky Mountains for the first time.

Have you ever found something unexpected and unexpectedly wonderful? Perhaps you were looking for something rather ordinary and vanilla, but what you found was something much more extraordinary. Perhaps you were not looking for anything in particular but came across something wonderful completely by accident.

Jesus told two parables in Matt 13:44–46 that describe such discoveries. The first parable is as follows: "The kingdom of heaven is like treasure hidden in a field. When a man found it, he hid it again, and then in his joy went and sold all he had and bought that field."

The second parable follows immediately after the first: "Again, the kingdom of heaven is like a merchant looking for fine pearls. When he found one of great value, he went away and sold everything he had and bought it." Some imagine a wealthy connoisseur, painstakingly working his way through a large collection of pearls of various sizes and value. His expert eyes survey the precious spheres, analyzing and assessing each and every one until he spots that one pearl of greater value than all the rest; one he would sell all he has to obtain. Dodd asks whether it was "unpardonable rashness . . . [to sell all and] buy a single pearl."[95]

The parables must be observed together, evidenced by the word "again" in verse 45, which implies that the second parable expresses something similar to what is found in the first parable.[96] The parables share the same plot, which is seen in the sequence of finding, selling, and buying.[97] These verbs, benign in and of themselves, become indicative of how the life of this man is forever changed. Simple and common under normal circumstances, in the parable the acts are mile markers along a road to a life that will never be the same. Second, they share the thrill of discovery. Even though the man accidentally discovers the treasure, and the merchant intentionally searches for and discovers the pearl, each

---

95. Dodd, *Parables of the Kingdom*, 85.

96. Long, *Preaching and the Literary Forms*, 104.

97. Crossan, *In Parables*, 34.

share the thrill of something unexpected: the man finds treasure he did not expect, and the merchant finds a pearl he did not anticipate. Third, each parable implies a change in the future of the man who finds the treasure and the merchant who finds the pearl.

The thrill and joy of discovery emerges in the telling of these parables. Jesus explains the purpose of the parables is to explain what the kingdom of heaven is like: the kingdom of heaven is like treasure hidden in a field and the kingdom of heaven is like a merchant looking for fine pearls. The parables state that the kingdom of heaven "is like" the situations described in their story of finding-selling-buying. In other words, the point is not that the kingdom of heaven is like treasure or a highly valuable pearl, but that it is like the finding of treasure in a field and the reality of a pearl more valuable than any other. All of this leads to the sense of searching and the promise of discovery.

What makes discovery exciting is when what is discovered is significant; otherwise, we have merely found something, and that discovery is of little consequence. It is like finding a dime or a quarter on the sidewalk, not very significant and certainly not very exciting. Such a discovery is of no consequence.

An Ethiopian treasurer made a discovery of consequence, similar perhaps in a way to that of the merchant in the second of our parables. A Jewish proselyte, he was returning from Jerusalem and was engaged in reading a scroll of the prophet Isaiah (Acts 8:27–28). The disciple Philip approached, and the Ethiopian told him that he was unsure of what he read, wondering about whom the prophet spoke, himself or another.

Learning the dilemma of the Ethiopian, Philip "preached Jesus to him" (8:35). At some point along the way, the Ethiopian was convinced of his need for baptism and upon completion of his immersion, "went on his way rejoicing" (8:36, 38–39). In his search for answers as a Jewish proselyte, having worshipped in the holy city of Jerusalem, the Ethiopian discovered more than he had hoped for; he discovered the salvation of Jesus Christ. It is wonderful when we find more than we expected, when the discovery makes the search so wonderfully worthwhile.

A key to these parables is the selling of all the two men possessed. Dodd suggests that at first what the merchant did might appear to be "unpardonable rashness," yet quickly adds that "to know when to plunge makes the successful financier. . . . You must feel quite sure of the value of the property you are buying."[98]

The point then may be the evidence of true discipleship that allows one to sacrifice whatever is necessary to obtain the kingdom of heaven.[99] The apostle Paul knew this very well, for he had much of what a good Jew would desire: heritage, education, and authority. Paul, however, "sold" all he had as bragging rights in the Jewish world to obtain the "excellence of the knowledge of Christ Jesus my Lord . . . that I may gain Christ" (Phil 3:8). In spite of his former accolades, Paul realized the eternal value of being a disciple of Jesus Christ.

What are we willing to "sell" to obtain the kingdom of heaven? The answer may not be as obvious as some might assume, for there are many things people would evidently choose to hold on to rather than obtain the kingdom of heaven. Jesus insisted, "It is hard for a rich man to enter into the kingdom of heaven" and "it is easier for a camel to go through the eye of a needle than for a rich man to enter the kingdom of God" (Matt 19:23–24). A rich man demonstrated this to Jesus when he asked the Lord what he had to do to obtain eternal life. When told of the price—sell all he had and give it to the poor—he was very sad, for he was very wealthy (Luke 18:18–23).

This is why the kingdom of heaven is like finding something so extraordinary as hidden treasure and a pearl of tremendous value; when one discovers its true worth, he is willing to give up all else to obtain it. Peter once was willing to claim he did not even know Jesus (Matt 26:69–75). He eventually came to discover, however, that he and all other disciples of Jesus Christ have been given living hope through an inheritance incorruptible, undefiled, unfading, and fitted with a reservation card in heaven (1 Pet 1:3–4).

So, the search is on and all of us will participate. Some will search for things only significant in the values of the world, such as educational degrees, cures for illness, and remedies for social dysfunction and in doing so seek after what is admirable. Others will intentionally search for spiritual things. Some will seek out the theologies of popular opinion and the practices of the status quo. A few will find the greatest story ever told and its incredible, undeniable, and unsurpassable value. It is the story of the kingdom of heaven, and they are able to see it in its magnificence.

98. Dodd, *Parables of the Kingdom*, 85.

99. Blomberg, "Preaching the Parables," 133.

It is within our nature as human beings to pay any price to obtain what we really want, what is most significant to us: parents who spend any amount of money, time, and effort for their children or the Olympic athlete who invests thousands of hours of tedious and demanding training to represent his or her country and win a medal. In the movie *The Day after Tomorrow*[100] the world is faced with every sort of weather catastrophe known to humans at a magnitude not seen in thousands of years. When separated by geography and danger, one of the main characters in the movie proclaims to his son, "I will come for you; whatever it takes, I will come for you." The movie then focuses on the father's perilous journey to make sure his son is safe.

How far are we willing to go to find the kingdom of heaven? What price are we willing to pay to obtain such treasure, something of such incredible value? What do we cherish so much that we would be unwilling to give up possessing the kingdom of heaven?

It is time to give up the world and seek after the priceless treasure of the kingdom of heaven.

The Parable of the Good Samaritan (Luke 10:30–37)

The parable of the good Samaritan, which is peculiar to Luke,[101] is perhaps one of the most familiar of all the parables of Jesus. Blomberg points out that what might be found in this passage is actually two "halves" that "parallel each other closely."[102] Bernard Scott carries this thought even further by pointing out "for many commentators" the shift from the neighbor being "someone I must love" (verses 27 and 29) to the neighbor being "someone who shows mercy" (verse 31) indicates "the parable and the Lukan context were originally separate."[103]

The question of the lawyer, "Who is my neighbor?" is central to the interpretation of this parable. While this parable is unique to Luke, the command to love God and to love one's neighbor is certainly not unique.

---

100. Emmerich, *Day After Tomorrow*, 58 min.

101. Both Craddock (*Luke*, 149) and Crossan (*In Parables*, 57–58) point out similarities to the question of eternal life in this parable and what is found in Matt 22:34–40 and Mark 12:28–31. Crossan also offers a comparison of Luke 10:30–37 to a similar story in the Gospel of Thomas.

102. Blomberg, *Interpreting the Parables*, 230.

103. Scott, *Hear Then the Parable*, 192.

Craddock points out that the parable joins the two commands, to love God (Deut 6:5) and to love one's neighbor (Lev 19:18), and their acknowledgement by Jesus supports those commands.[104] The interpretation of the command to love one's neighbor is the function of the parable in Lukan theology.[105] The question anticipates the larger task of identifying that duty of man that leads to eternal life, namely charity. Bernard Scott points out that the parable parallels the account of the rich ruler's inquiry of obtaining eternal life in Matt 18:18. In this way, says Scott, "when the question recurs" in the inquiry of the ruler, the reader is forced to read the answer in light of what occurs in Jesus' encounter with the lawyer (Luke 10:25).[106]

The parable has been called a "controversy dialogue,"[107] in fact a "double controversy dialogue," containing two parallel components: first, the lawyer's question, Jesus' counterquestion, the lawyer's answer, and Jesus' command (10:25–28), and second, then the same pattern is repeated (10:29-37). The two parts form the double controversy, each following the same dialogue pattern and ending with the command of Jesus to do as commanded. It is the second question of the lawyer, "Who is my neighbor?" that forms the reason for the parable.

Tension is formed by the conduct of the three main characters: a priest and a Levite, as well as a Samaritan. The actions of the priest and Levite, who see what has happened and pass by, are contrasted to that of the Samaritan, who sees what has happened and acts out of charity for the fallen man. This contrast and so the tension that arises from it is intentional on the part of Jesus.[108]

It might be too critical to lay blame upon the priest and Levite. Returning from their duties in Jerusalem, they would have spotted the unfortunate man and possibly believed him to be dead, for he was perhaps lying motionless. Blomberg, Scott, and Jeremias[109] point out that it would be against Jewish law for the priest to touch the victim if he were dead. The law clearly stated in Lev 21:1–11 that a priest was not to touch a dead body, even in everyday life. Yet, Jeremias is quick to ask why the Levite did not

---

104. Craddock, *Luke*, 150.

105. Talbert, *Reading Luke*, 120.

106. Scott, *Hear Then the Parable*, 191.

107. Talbert, *Reading Luke*, 120.

108. Jeremias, *Parables*, 204.

109. Jeremias, *Parables*, 203.

assist the unfortunate man, for no such restrictions were laid upon Levites except in their duties in the temple.[110]

The literary structure of the passage lends itself to identify three distinct parts: (1) the priest and the Levite "sharing one role as the negative model," (2) the Samaritan "providing the shocking counter example," and (3) "the determining figure [of] the man in the ditch."[111] Jeremias notices this pattern as well, commenting that it follows "the triadic form of popular stories," making the audience expect the arrival of a third character, "an Israelite layman," for the audience would have expected the parable to have "an anti-clerical point."[112] The hero then is one whom the listener/reader would not expect: the non-Jew, the Samaritan.

The instruction of Jesus to go and do likewise indicates the parable's focus on what the lawyer and those like him should do. While mercy and compassion are perfected in the life of Jesus, this parable is intended to illustrate what was missing in the heart of the lawyer who asked the identity of his neighbor out of self-justification.[113]

So then, the question, "Who is my neighbor?" becomes the focus of the parable. Bernard Scott points out that some reject neighborliness as the point of the parable, emphasizing instead the question, "Who showed mercy on him" that comes at the end of the parable.[114] The question implies selectivity; a desire to choose whom one would love as a neighbor.

That which saves is not found in a single virtue, but in the combination of love, compassion, and faithful action. This parable expresses Jesus' teaching on the two greatest commandments: first, to love God, and then second, to love your neighbor as yourself. Jesus encourages the listener/ reader of the parable to do as the Samaritan, for in doing so we will receive eternal life. The kingdom is implied in the parable, then, for it embodies God's universal love and not a love of partiality.

Preaching the Parable of the Good Samaritan as Vessel

What would a sermon about the good Samaritan look like if it were preached as a vessel? Unlike the parables of the hidden treasure and the pearl (Matt

---

110. Jeremias, *Parables*, 203–204.

111. Blomberg, *Interpreting the Parables*, 232.

112. Jeremias, *Parables*, 204.

113. Talbert, *Reading Luke*, 122.

114. Scott, *Hear Then the Parable*, 191.

13:44–46), which revealed themselves in an obvious way through "the kingdom of heaven is like" statements that begin each one, the parable of the good Samaritan does not contain such a statement.

However, the vessel parable is not marked only by an "is like" statement. In addition to the language of comparison and contrast, which we saw in preaching the parables of the treasure and the pearl, the vessel parable also employs the device of "end stress" with "an emphasis upon the final episode and its implied meaning."[115]

The parable of the good Samaritan is an example of the vessel's "end stress." Therefore, the vessel sermon below differs from the object of art sermon that follows it: the former focuses on the "end stress" of the arrival and conduct of the Samaritan and how he illustrates Jesus' teaching of love and being a neighbor, while the object of art sermon draws the listener into the story as they associate themselves with the plot and characters.

As a vessel parable, the good Samaritan is built around a series of events, the first of two or more occurring in a similar manner. This is seen in the actions of the priest and the Levite. When the final and climactic events occur, the actions of the Samaritan, something different emerges "and this is where the rhetorical spotlight falls."[116]

As a vessel sermon on this parable, the focus will also be the message to be learned, occurring toward the end of the sermon itself. Before that is done, however, the sermon will relate the story and, in doing so, ask the listener several questions and make several observations that are intended to direct the listener toward the message. All of that is a part of the pedagogical nature of the vessel parable and so then the vessel sermon. A vessel sermon seeks to explain the deeper reality contained within the symbolism of the parable.

A sermon preached on the parable of the good Samaritan as vessel or simile might look like the following.

"Acting like a Samaritan"

Sometimes we just have a bad day when things go wrong and there is not much we can do to stop it. Perhaps it is just being in the wrong place, at the wrong time. Perhaps these things just happen. Some claim it is a sign of modern times while others blame bad things that happen to good people on

---

115. Long, *Preaching and the Literary Forms*, 99.

116. Long, *Preaching and the Literary Forms*, 99.

the moral deterioration of our society.[117] So it was for a man on a day in the first century, according to a parable of Jesus in Luke 10:30–37.

A man had approached Jesus with a question: "What must I do to inherit eternal life?" (Luke 10:25). The NIV refers to the man as an "expert in the law," while other translations[118] simply call him a "lawyer." Either rendering is suitable, but the former is perhaps a bit more descriptive. We might ask why "a learned theologian should ask a layman about the way to eternal life" adding that doing so "was just as unusual then as it would be today."[119]

New Testament scholar Joachim Jeremias proposes that the preaching of Jesus caused the man to be "disturbed in conscience."[120] While that may be the case, it is also sensible to assume the lawyer had something other than an act of conscience in mind. Considering that the man is an expert in the law, why does he not know the answer to the question? Is he simply unaware of what the law states on the matter or does he have some ulterior motive for asking Jesus the question?

Regardless of the man's intentions, Jesus ignored the implications and asked the man what the law said. The legal expert, alluding to Deut 6:5, replied that one must love the Lord with all of one's heart, soul, strength, and mind, as well as loving one's neighbor as yourself (Luke 10:25–27). Jesus commended the man for answering correctly, instructing him to love his neighbor as himself and he would live (eternally) (Luke 10:28).

At first glance this confrontation appeared to have gone rather well, for often Jesus and the Jewish leaders clashed. The two agreed and that seems to be very positive. For once, one of the Jewish leaders evidently did not seek to trap, ridicule, or humiliate Jesus in some way. Yet, the man was not finished, and he evidently did have an ulterior motive, for he continued the inquiry, seeking to justify himself by asking the identity of his neighbor (Luke 10:29). It is a rather loaded question, perhaps with implications of selectivity. In other words, his neighbor is who he chooses, namely another Jew. After all, every Jew knows he can associate only with Jews.

How would he justify himself by asking the question? Probably it is in conjunction with his first question, desiring to show evidence of his contemplation and practice of what leads to eternal life. Yet, it is highly likely

---

117. Blomberg, "Preaching the Parables," 60.

118. For example, the KJV, NKJV, and NRSV.

119. Jeremias, *Parables*, 202.

120. Jeremias, *Parables*, 202.

that his question was not intended merely to receive instruction, but to validate his own sense of self-justification. Asking a question to gain an advantage over another "is not a kingdom exercise," nor is doing so with no intention of practicing what the answer implies.[121]

So then, the lawyer's desire for self-justification comes in three steps. First, he approached Jesus, addressing him as "Teacher," to inquire of eternal matters. Second, he established his knowledge of the law by his quotation of it and Jesus' acknowledgement of his correct answer. Third, he sought to appear pious and benevolent by inquiring the identity of his neighbor, as if to say, "So I am assured to do it correctly."

It is in response to the second question, "Who is my neighbor?" that Jesus proclaims the parable known as the "good Samaritan." The story is perhaps one of the most familiar of all the parables of Jesus.

A man was traveling toward the city of Jericho from Jerusalem when he was attacked, robbed, and very badly injured. As he lay there, stripped of his clothing, someone approached along the same road. It was a priest, probably headed toward Jericho just as was the victim. This is the victim's lucky day, for a priest of God will certainly stop and help. However, the priest saw the wounded man and passed by him on the other side of the road.

A man of God is not supposed to do that, is he? Is he not expected to help his fellow man? Does he not know the law as the lawyer knows it; does he not know to love his neighbor as he loves himself (Lev 19:18)? Yet, he did not help, but ignored the plight of the man on the road. Yet wait, the priest may believe the man to be dead and, therefore, untouchable according to Jewish law. With that information one might be able to excuse the priest for what appears to be an evident lack of concern.[122]

A little later a Levite approaches on the road and he saw the wounded man as well, but also passes by on the other side of the road. This servant in the temple should be expected to know the law and so then help another, but he did as the priest and ignored the circumstances that had befallen the unfortunate man. However, unlike the priest, the Levite is not restricted from touching the body of a dead man except in the performance of his duties in the temple.[123]

Will no one help this poor man, lying naked and badly injured on the side of the road between Jerusalem and Jericho? The city of Jericho boasted

---

121. Craddock, *Luke*, 150.

122. Jeremias, *Parables*, 203.

123. Jeremias, *Parables*, 203–4.

a large population of priests and Levites, so many would be passing by on their way home. Surely one of them will care enough to help and not pass by the wounded man on the other side of this heavily traveled road.

Another man approaches on the same road, but this time it is a Samaritan. The Samaritans and Jews are enemies, so one might wonder what he will do to this unfortunate man. Indeed, this is not this poor man's lucky day. Not only is he left to die by two of his fellow countrymen, and a priest and a Levite at that, but a Samaritan now approaches him, and every Jew knows what sort of people they are.

But wait, what do we see? The Samaritan stops and bends over the wounded man. Something is not right about this, for the Samaritan does not appear to have anything criminal in mind. He helps the wounded man by pouring a mixture of oil and wine, commonly used for medicinal purposes in this period of time, and dressed his wounds. This is truly amazing; a Samaritan dressing the wounds of a Jew. His care shows his love for his fellow man, even if his fellow man is a Jew. The wounded man is then placed on the Samaritan's own donkey and is taken to a nearby inn. Will the Samaritan leave the man there and continue on his way? He has already done more than anyone would expect, so he could not be blamed for continuing his travels. The Samaritan does not continue on, however, but stays at the inn to take care of the man. The next day the Samaritan pays the innkeeper two silver coins and arranges for the wounded man to receive further care, promising to reimburse the innkeeper for all his expenses.

When Jesus finished the parable, he asked the expert in the law "who in the story was a neighbor to the man who had fallen victim to robbers." The lawyer replied, "The one who had mercy on him" (Luke 10:37). Jesus instructed the legal expert to go and do the same.

What is the message of this parable? From whom are we to learn the message: the Samaritan who was "good," the victim, the priest, or the Levite?[124] Is this a parable about being a good neighbor or is there more to it than that? After all, Jesus told the parable in response to loving God with all one's heart, soul, strength, and mind, as well as loving one's neighbor as oneself (Luke 10:27).

---

124. Craddock (*Luke*, 151) warns against "painting unnecessarily unattractive portraits of the priest and the Levite," for doing so "greatly weakens the story." Realism is essential to the audience being able to identify with the characters and if the priest and Levite are depicted as "ethically dead and totally devoid of human caring, then no listener will say, 'I too have behaved that way.'"

Perhaps the point of the parable goes deeper than just being neighborly. This is where we come to realize the "aha!" of a vessel sermon, for now we can see what is hidden beneath the surface: the form of the vessel sermon has pointed the listener toward that message. Recall that the expert in the law asked about obtaining eternal life, to which Jesus responded by reciting the parable, along with the command to go and do likewise. Jesus wanted the legal expert to do what likewise? Perhaps Jesus wanted to impress upon the lawyer just how to obtain eternal life. If the law says that one is to love God and love one's neighbor, then to love one's neighbor is to also love God. As the song states, "Love one another, for love is of God." Such love leads to eternal life.

This sort of love, however, is not just affection. We are never just to have affection for God, something casual and limited in its scope. David loved God because of what the Lord had done for him (Pss 31:23; 116:1). This indicated a relationship with God and that led to David's committed love. So, it is when one loves a neighbor. It is not a casual or convenient love, but the love of a commitment to another human being. The Samaritan probably did not know the Jew he aided, but he knew the plight of a fellow human being and the relationship of that empathy.

The neighborly nature of the Samaritan reflected what Jesus wanted the people to know about him and what they should reflect in themselves. So, when the legal expert asked what he had to do to inherit eternal life, Jesus responded with reflection on the law. When the legal expert pushed it further, asking the identity of his neighbor, Jesus followed up with a story of how that aspect of the law is evidenced.

"Go and do likewise" is also said to each of us, for we are to love God with all of our heart, soul, strength, and mind, loving our neighbor as ourselves (Matt 22:37). Such practices are not to be done for self-justification, but to reveal the will of God in how we show mercy and love to others. This very basic but powerful point became an essential point in the building of the church, for it established the desire of Jesus that his church would be a spiritual community that is open to all. In order for us to be that community, everyone around us is our neighbor.

So, who will be your neighbor? To whom will you show the type of love Jesus wants? Who will "go and do likewise" and be a "good Samaritan?" The result is putting into practice what Jesus desires for his church. In fact, the result is eternal life.

Preaching the Parable of the Good Samaritan As Object of Art

How does a sermon about the good Samaritan look if it is preached as an "object of art"? As I mentioned above in the examination of preaching the parables of the hidden treasure and the pearl (Matt 13:44–46), through its plot the object of art sermon seeks to draw the reader/listener into the world of the parable.[125] It does not attempt to explain anything, as the vessel sermon does; the object of art sermon seeks to move the reader/listener toward an interaction with the characters in the parable.

It may not be an exaggeration to say that the parable of the good Samaritan allows the reader/listener to be drawn into its plot more than any other object of art parable. While it is by no means the only object of art parable (I examined the parables of the hidden treasure and the pearl [Matt 13:44–46] as objects of art), the unexpected twists and irony within the good Samaritan causes the reader/listener to be surprised through a story that unfolds unexpectedly. The reader/listener is made to wonder, "What would I have done?" It is the element of shock and surprise, combined with the personal reflection of the listener that separates the object of art sermon from that of the vessel. The object of art sermon focuses on the reactions of the listener, while the vessel sermon drives the listener toward seeing the deeper meaning underneath the symbolism. The object of art sermon seeks to draw the listener into the story itself, then, forces a reaction.

In this sermon on the good Samaritan, I will repeat the question, "Can you imagine?" as it is applied to the characters in the story. Instead of a mere learning experience, such as in the vessel sermon where I directed the listener toward the parable's meaning, the object of art sermon emerges as a personal experience: "Would I have done that?" The listener is intended to sense the feelings of the priest, Levite, Samaritan, and the victim; the listener is put into their place. That is not to say the vessel and object of art sermons on the good Samaritan do not have similarities. First, both unpack the story, but do so in different ways: the vessel sermon unpacks the story for the listener and directs him or her toward a conclusion, while the object of art sermon allows the listener to unpack the story through personal reflection. Second, in unpacking the story, both the vessel and object of art sermons focus on the highlights of the story: the inquiry of the legal expert, the plight of the victim, the reactions of the priest

---

125. Long, *Preaching and the Literary Forms*, 105.

and Levite, and the compassion of the Samaritan. Third, both the vessel and object of art sermons emphasize the message Jesus taught, "go and do likewise" (Luke 10:37): the vessel sermon teaches the listener to go and do likewise, while the object of art sermon allows the listener to imagine what it would be like to act as the loving and neighborly Samaritan.

When the parable of the good Samaritan is preached as an object of art, it might look like the following.

"Can You Imagine Anyone Doing Something like That?"

Jesus was confronted and questioned by many throughout his ministry. Overall, their primary purpose was the same: they wished to catch him in a contradiction (e.g., Mark 12:13) and, so, discredit him as the prophet, teacher, and the Christ he claimed to be. This was the case in Luke 10 when an expert in the law asked Jesus, "Teacher, what shall I do to inherit eternal life?" (10:25). As was the case so many times, the text indicates the legal expert asked this question to test Jesus. Jesus responded to the question by asking a question of his own: "What is written in the law? What is your reading of it?" (10:26). The legal expert alluded to Deut 6:5 and Lev 19:18, stating one should love God with all his heart, soul, strength, and mind, as well as love his neighbor as himself (10:27). Hearing the response, Jesus indicated that the legal expert had answered correctly and encouraged him to "do this and you will live" (10:28).

The legal expert was not finished, however, but pushed the situation even further. He had originally desired to test Jesus by asking the question of inheriting eternal life. Now he sought to justify himself by asking, "Who is my neighbor?" (10:29). In essence, due to the Jewish recognition of only other Jews as covenant people, the lawyer's question is basically, "Who belongs to the category of God's people?"[126]

In what way did the legal expert seek to justify himself with his inquiry of his neighbor? Perhaps, he felt himself justified because he felt he would be seen as a man who contemplated the quest of eternal life and the depths of Jewish law. Perhaps he also would feel justified if he were able to trap Jesus in something compromising or false. Since his first question did not prove successful, he tried again with the question of how the law regarding loving one's neighbor would be applied. It is as if he asked, "If I am to love my neighbor, I need to know who my neighbor is."

126. Talbert, *Reading Luke*, 121.

Instead of addressing the question directly, Jesus launches into a parable about a man traveling from Jerusalem to Jericho. The parable does not indicate the purpose of the man's journey toward Jericho, whether it was his final destination or a stop along the way. Regardless of his intentions, he is somewhere along the road toward the city of Jericho. The man is attacked, robbed, stripped of his clothing, and left half dead along the side of the road (Luke 10:30).

Fortunately, this is a well-traveled road, so it is not long before someone comes along. It is a priest, probably traveling to his home in Jericho, having finished his duties in the temple.[127] Upon seeing the unfortunate man, however, the priest passes by on the other side of the road (10:31). Can you imagine him, a priest, doing that? A little while later a Levite is also traveling along the road, also headed home after fulfilling his duties in Jerusalem, and approaches the wounded man, comes over to look, and he too passes by on the other side of the road (10:32). Can you imagine him, a Levite, doing that?

I remember reading of a violent assault committed in New York City in the early 1960s. A young woman was beaten and stabbed numerous times while her cries for help carried out of her window and down onto the street. The tragedy was compounded by dozens of people who passed by, hearing her cries for help, but did nothing, some even crossing to the other side of the street. A few stopped and looked toward the window from where the cries came, but then walked on, doing nothing. The public outcry was tremendous, both for the crime and for the lack of concern for another human being.

If you could be a spectator of these two events, separated by time and space, you might look on incredulously at the apparent lack of concern and compassion of the priest and Levite. As you watch them pass by the unfortunate man, you might feel the hopelessness and carelessness of the situation: someone has been hurt and no one will help him. Can you imagine anyone doing something like that?

Sometime after, a Samaritan approaches the man and had compassion on him. Ironic, is it not, that it is a Samaritan, an enemy of Israel, and not a Jew who comes to the man's aid. He first treated the man's wounds by pouring on oil and wine, sometimes used medicinally at that time.

Then, the Samaritan set the man on his animal and brought him to a local inn and took care of him through the night. Leaving the inn the

127. Blomberg, "Preaching the Parables," 61.

next day, the Samaritan gave the innkeeper two denarii with instructions to care for the wounded man, promising to reimburse the innkeeper upon his return (10:32–36).

Concluding the parable, Jesus asked the lawyer which of the three men in the parable was a neighbor to the wounded man (10:36). The legal expert replied that it was the one who showed mercy on the wounded man. Jesus instructed him to go and do likewise (10:37). Imagine being that unfortunate person on the road between Jerusalem and Jericho. What would it be like to fall prey to robbers, stripped, and left to die? Imagine the emotional experience the victim felt if he were conscious and saw a priest and then a Levite approaching, only to pass by without doing anything to help. As a Jew, he would be able to depend on his fellow Jews, especially those who serve in the temple, wouldn't he? We have already seen how the law commanded them to love God and their neighbor as they would themselves (Lev 19:18). Yet they failed to do anything at all.

Imagine also being the victim, a Jew, and seeing a Samaritan approaching. Yes, a Samaritan, an enemy and one who is considered off limits to any good Jew. Yet it is a Samaritan and not a Jew who helps, not only tending to your wounds but also spending the night caring for your needs. Then, to top it all off, he leaves money (is a Samaritan's money any good?) for any further care that might be required.

Am I being too critical of the priest and Levite? After all, the robbers who attacked the man in the first place may have been hiding nearby waiting for another victim of their treachery. Is that not what the majority would do?[128] Imagine walking the streets of a major city at night and spotting a person lying in an alley battered, bruised, and bloody. Would you rush to his aid, or would you suddenly adopt an "it's none of my business" frame of mind? How popular has such thinking become in our present world? Perhaps we can understand why the priest and Levite passed by on the other side.

Imagine how the Samaritan felt as he approached the wounded man. Why he is traveling on the road between Jerusalem and Jericho is left to speculation, but whatever the reason for him being there at that time, his arrival was beneficial for the Jew. What was he thinking as he approached the man? Did he also wonder if the robbers were nearby or

---

128. Blomberg, "Preaching the Parables," 61. Blomberg adds that the priest and Levite also might have thought the man to be dead and so then unclean. Jeremias offers a similar point (*Parables*, 203).

did his compassion for a wounded human override his fear of being attacked? Did he consider the implications of a Samaritan being seen beside a wounded Jew? Did he care one way or the other?

It has been popular in times past to ask the question, "What would Jesus do?" The question became a phenomenon among the Christian youth of our nation a few years ago as they displayed the initials "WWJD?" on shirts, posters, wristbands, key chains, and just about anything else on which the slogan could be imprinted. While the question, "What would Jesus do?" raises an interesting and significant point, perhaps a better question to ask is, "What *did* Jesus do?" The answer to the question is rather obvious, of course, for his very purpose, as the Great Physician, was to come to the aid of his neighbor. Yet, his purpose was spiritual and not physical. As he went in search of the spiritually ill, did he do so to neglect those in physical need?

We do not really talk much about it, do we? We focus so much on his mission as Lord and Savior but fail to determine how he might have treated his neighbor. Little, if any evidence is given in the Gospels of Jesus bending to pick up one who had fallen, offering a drink of water to the thirsty, or, as in the parable, coming to the aid of a victim of violence. Yet, Jesus spoke of such things throughout his ministry. His encouragement to love one's neighbor as himself is not isolated to the dialogue between him and the legal expert. In Matt 5:43–48 he upset the apple cart of common social thinking by insisting that not only is one to love his neighbor, but he was to love his enemies as well. After all, Jesus adds, if you love only those who love you, how is that different than anyone else? To Jesus, love was more than just something convenient, but something extraordinary. Jesus displayed his concern for others in his love for children. He loved the innocence and humility of a child (Matt 18:2–4) and sought to protect them because of that. At one point, as he spoke to his disciples, he took a child in his arms and, offering welcome to another, proclaimed that anyone who welcomed a child also welcomed him (Matt 18:5; Mark 9:36–37), but then warned that anyone who harmed one of them would be better off drowned in the sea (Matt 18:6).

Throughout his preaching and teaching among the multitudes Jesus constantly encouraged them to look out for others, such as doing to others as you would have them do to you, what has been called the "Golden Rule" (Matt 7:12). This corresponds with his instructions to the multitudes to not resist an evil person but turn the other cheek and go the extra mile for another (Matt 5:38–42). Do we see this very thing in action when he was struck but did not retaliate against his accusers and attackers (Matt 26:67; Mark 14:65; Luke 22:63–65; John 18:22)? Perhaps he did not strike back because these were some he would later ask his Father to forgive, for they did not know what they were doing (Luke 23:34). You see, even in his trying hours, he was concerned for the welfare of others.

In this way, Jesus is the epitome of what he emphasizes in the character and practice of the Samaritan: Jesus loved his neighbor as he loved himself. Let us make the point again: imagine being the priest, Levite, or the Samaritan. To be as the priest or Levite is in contradiction to what Jesus evidenced in his own life, but to be the Samaritan was to be as Jesus, caring for another, regardless of who that person might be.

Who is your neighbor? It is more than a question of fellowship and acceptance, but one that reveals the righteousness of the Lord and his command to love God with your heart, soul, strength, and mind, and to love your neighbor as your own self. The Samaritan displayed love, concern, and compassion for the unfortunate man on the side of the road. When others did nothing, he stopped and did what he could. Can you imagine anyone doing that? The one who loves his neighbor as himself would do that. The one who desires eternal life would do that. The one who wishes to emulate the Lord Jesus Christ would do that.

We must "go and do likewise," for in doing so we reflect what is of Jesus Christ and we continue our journey out of this world to inherit eternal life. Can you imagine anyone doing that? Yes, we will do that, and we will go home.

The Parable of the Sower (Mark 4:1–9, 13–20; Luke 8:4–8)

Unlike the other two parables of this study,[129] the parable of the sower is found in more than one passage of Scripture: Mark 4:1–9,13–20 and Luke 8:4–8, 11–15.[130] The parable illuminates a spiritual truth through a means known by all, a farmer sowing seed in his field, something most would have seen regularly.[131] The parable depicts the casting of seed onto a field

---

129. I am including the parables of the hidden treasure and the pearl as one parable. Even though they are two parables, they are read as on in this study. Of course, the good Samaritan would be the second parable.

130. The parable of the Sower is also found in Matt 13, but I am focusing on the Mark 4 and Luke 8 accounts.

131. English, *Message of Mark*, 93.

and the variety of places on which the seed lands. In spite of the reader/ listener's familiarity with the process of sowing, the use of that image is unusual and begs explanation. "The hearer has a feeling of strangeness in a very familiar narrative," writes Craddock, "and some interpretation is not only invited but urged."[132]

For the most part Mark and Luke tell the story in the same way: a sower scatters seeds in the field and some seed falls on the path, some on the rocky soil, some among the thorns, and some on the good, fertile ground. Also in both accounts, the meaning of the parable is the same, indicating those who hear but the devil intercedes (the path), those who hear but the word takes no root (rocky soil), those who hear but the concerns of the world intercede (thorns), and those who hear, accept, and retain the word (good soil).

The two accounts differ also in a few points. The parable in Mark follows the healing of a man with a shriveled hand (3:1–6), the healing of the diseases of the multitudes (3:7–12), the appointment of the twelve apostles (3:13–19), the Jews claiming Jesus was possessed by Beelzebub (3:20–30), and the arrival of Jesus' mother and brothers (Mark 3:34–35).

On the other hand, Luke places the parable in the larger context, after the account of the sinful woman who washed the feet of Jesus with her tears and dried them with her hair (Luke 7:36–50). Immediately preceding the parable Jesus is said to have been traveling "from one town and village to another proclaiming the good news of the kingdom of God" with the twelve apostles and a number of women who "were helping to support them out of their own means" (Luke 8:1–2).

Immediately preceding the parable, Mark's account emphasizes Jesus was so pressed by the multitudes he had to preach to them from a boat on the lake (Mark 4:1). Luke, on the other hand, makes no mention of the boat, but portrays Jesus first proclaiming the good news and curing the people of evil spirits and diseases before preaching the parable.

This became a moral situation, the parable is told to call the people toward self-examination that has arisen in the midst of what could be seen as enthusiasm, for the multitude is so large Jesus had to take refuge in a boat on the lake. Scott emphasizes the process of Jesus actually sitting in the boat, indicating that doing so may recall Ps 29:10: "The Lord sits enthroned over the flood; the Lord is enthroned as King forever."[133]

132. Craddock, *Luke*, 108.

133. Scott, *Hear Then the Parable*, 346.

One final difference between Mark and Luke in the telling of the parable of the sower is found in the description of the seed falling on the good soil. Mark wrote that the seed was multiplied thirty, sixty, or one hundred times, while Luke multiplied the seed only one hundred times. In spite of this variation, both accounts reflect an extremely high amount.

Donald English places the point of emphasis at Mark 4:8, where the seed falls on good ground, yielding a crop multiplied thirty, sixty, or even one hundred times.[134] In this way, the receptivity of the ground becomes a central focus of the parable, for the ground's receptivity becomes a determining factor of the harvest.[135]

Talbert, in making the point about the various responses to the word, wonders why there was such a lasting response in so few.[136] Jesus explains in Mark 4:14–19 why the responses were remarkably negative: the devil (roadside), temptations (rocks), and worldly cares (thorns). The point of the parable, to borrow from Dodd's "the kingdom of God is like this" interpretation of parables,[137] is "a truth related to the kingdom of God," which English suggests is an explanation of why some respond and enter the kingdom and others do not.[138] Those who do not enter the kingdom neglect to do so due to human hardness, shallowness, and self-indulgence.

Preaching the Parable of the Sower as Code

A central purpose of parables that function as code is they match "each major aspect of the parable to a corresponding element in that deeper but hidden reality."[139] The parable of the sower does this rather nicely, matching a variety of four different soils to a variety of attitudes toward the word of God as it is proclaimed.

Another function of the parables of code is they contain one detail that does not fit with the rest of the story. This process is intended to disrupt the flow of the parable.[140] At first glance, the parable of the sower

---

134. English, *Message of Mark*, 93.

135. English, *Message of Mark*, 94.

136. Talbert, *Reading Luke*, 3–4

137. Dodd, *Parables of the Kingdom*, 132.

138. English, *Message of Mark*, 94.

139. Long, *Preaching and the Literary Forms*, 96.

140. Long (*Preaching and the Literary Forms*, 98–99) writes that the rhetorical effect of code is disruption, where something does not comfortably fit, or the situation falls

does not appear to offer such a disruption in the flow of its story. The story emerges as the casting of seed and the subsequent results of the sowing. Nothing in the story appears to disrupt what the reader might assume to be the act of sowing seed and reaping a harvest.

Closer examination reveals the parable finds its disruption, and so its identification as a parable of code, through what is not stated. For example, is the sower careless as he casts the seed about, allowing the majority of it to fall on soil unsuitable for a bountiful harvest? We are not to assume the seed that falls on the roadside and among the rocks and thorns represents the majority of the seed sown. As the reader/listener encounters the story, he might wonder to himself, "Why would this person do that? How could someone so careless expect any sort of success in the harvest?" The reader knows something is wrong and expects that knowledge to be confirmed. This is the focus of the code parable and sermon, to confirm, clarify, and certify what the reader/listener already knows, and everyone knows you cannot plant seed in such a way and expect a bountiful harvest.

This becomes the point of the parable and the sermon as well: only the right soil will produce a bountiful harvest; those who are the good soil inhabit the kingdom of heaven. The sermon that follows focuses on that simple concept. As the point of the parable and its preaching is discovered, the reader/listener is able to proclaim, "Ah, yes I know," and that is a thoroughly appropriate response to a code parable.

Presented as code, preaching the parable of the sower as code will focus on the issue of proclaiming the word of God and the response that will be made to such proclamation. The sermon will ask the question, "Who will be the right soil?" The answer, of course, confirms what the listener already knows: if one will hear and accept the word of God, he or she will be the right soil.

If preached as code, a sermon about the parable of the sower might emerge in the following way.

"Being the Right Soil"

What would it be like to be followed everywhere you go? Would it be intimidating or exciting? Perhaps it would be extremely annoying or perhaps it would become a bit euphoric, having all of that attention: the questions, the photographs, and the curiosity. In our modern culture it

---

outside of reality.

is the price of fame and notoriety, from which terms such as "paparazzi" have been coined.

Everyone followed Jesus wherever he went, some to listen to him and some to accuse him. He traveled from town to town, "proclaiming the good news of the kingdom of God" (Luke 8:1) and they followed him. They seemed to come from everywhere and their numbers grew. They wanted to hear what he had to say and see what he would do. Some were empowered by his teaching and by his very presence, while others were unsure what to make of this teacher and prophet. A few were threatened by him and became antagonists at almost every turn. They all were curious, however, and so they continued to follow him.

He taught them in parables (Mark 4:2), "the most characteristic element in the teaching of Jesus Christ as recorded in the Gospels."[141] They were stories that described people who bore a resemblance to the experience of his audience, reflecting what they did and how they felt. The people he described in his parables might live next door, down the street, or actually be them. So, they listened to him tell his parables and they reacted to them. Some were thrilled by what he said, while others were intimidated, believing he criticized them, which he did at times. A few were drawn toward faith because of the parables Jesus told, for they saw where they had failed or were lacking. Regardless of their reaction, they listened, and they followed Jesus wherever he went to hear what else he would say.

One particular day next to the Sea of Galilee he told them a parable about a farmer who went out to sow seed (Mark 4:3; Luke 8:5). As he cast the seed on the ground it fell in a variety of places. Some of it fell on the path next to the fertile soil. Instead of sinking into the furrows it just laid there on the surface and the birds came and ate the seed (Mark 4:4), and it was trampled by people walking nearby (Luke 8:5). Some of it fell on the rocks that had been thrown nearby as the farmer had cleared his field for planting (Mark 4:5; Luke 8:6). Seed seems to be able to germinate just about anywhere; in sidewalks, in parking lots, just about anywhere there is just the slightest bit of soil, but there was nothing for the roots to grow into, so the sun scorched them, and they withered (Mark 4:6; Luke 8:6). Some of the seed fell on soil that had wild thorns growing in it. The thorns choked the seed of necessary nourishment, so it did not grow (Mark 4:7; Luke 8:7). Is that not the way it is when we want something to grow? We want flowers and vegetables, but other, undesirable things grow as well. Finally, some,

141. Dodd, *Parables of the Kingdom*, 13.

probably most of the seed fell on soil prepared for planting and the result was a healthy, thriving harvest that, according to Mark's account, produced thirty, sixty, even a hundred times over (Mark 4:8), while Luke only speaks of a hundred-fold increase (Luke 8:8). This is what is supposed to happen, is it not? After the effort to prepare the soil for planting, the end result should be a plentiful harvest. It is disappointing, even devastating to spend that kind of time and effort only to see no harvest from the labor.

Jesus sought to persuade the people to focus on the point of the parable, for he instructed them, "He who has ears to hear, let him hear" (Mark 4:9; Luke 8:8). This was a way of calling them to attention. I had a teacher in college who would periodically proclaim, "Okay, now listen fellers," indicating he wanted us to pay attention to what he had said or was about to say. Jesus does the same thing when he instructed them that if they had ears to hear, they should hear what the parable said.

Jesus specifically wanted them to hear the richness of the message contained within the parable. There was something important for them to hear, hidden in the story of the seed and the soil it fell upon. Of course, the parable was not really about a farmer planting seed, but something much deeper and more important. Instead of the farmer or the seed, it is the soils that determine the parable's meaning.[142]

Jesus explained the parable (Mark 4:13–20; Luke 8:11–15). The seed is the word of God and the farmer, Jesus said, sows the word of God. The imagery is not isolated to the parables of Jesus. The apostle Paul used the casting of seed in this way, along with the watering of Apollos and the increase of God, to illustrate his work within the church in Corinth (1 Cor 3:6). Some people, Jesus insisted, are like the path where the seed fell because they hear the word spoken, but Satan comes and removes the word from them. Luke adds that the word had been planted in their hearts, but Satan, in taking the seed, removed their belief and, so then, their desire to be saved (Luke 8:12).

Jesus continued to unpack the parable by explaining the seed sown on the rocks. The rocky soil represents those who hear the word and receive its hearing with joy, but there is nothing in which the seed can take root: when problems arise (Mark 4:16) or at the "time of testing" (Luke 8:13) they fall away. Their spirituality and faith are so shallow and lacking in substance, the power of the message has nothing within which to germinate, and they become weak.

142. English, *Message of Mark*, 94.

We all know of circumstances when people do this very thing when conflict arises within the congregation. They leave, either to find another place where human frailties in a congregation are less wearisome or they cease all association with the church altogether. We are all familiar with this all-too-common phenomenon. "I wonder what happened to the Smiths," someone might ask a fellow member, "they were once so faithful."

Jesus went on to say the soil filled with thorns represents those who allow the worries of life to interfere with the desire for salvation. The burdens and pressures of life in this world become too overwhelming and they do not see the power of the Lord to heal the wounds and offer a remedy. Jesus anticipated such reactions when he warned the gathered crowds to seek the kingdom of God and his righteousness rather than worrying over the temporary things of human life (Matt 6:25–34).

So, then the thorny soil also represents the deceitfulness of wealth and the desires of human existence to push aside what level of faith and conviction they once had. When I was involved in evangelistic campaigns in Great Britain, we would inevitably have greater success among the poorer of their society rather than those of higher income brackets. Their money and prosperity pushed Christianity aside; they had no need for the Lord any longer. So, it is with those of the thorns, for they become too caught up in what is happening around them in the here and now to be concerned about the condition of their souls in the hereafter. Jesus warned his disciples of such concerns: "I have told these things, so that in me you may have peace. In this world you will have trouble. But take heart! I have overcome the world" (John 16:33).

Odd, don't you think, to cast precious seed all about where it will not produce anything resembling a productive harvest? Why spend the time to prepare soil for planting and then cast the seed wildly about where it falls on places not suited for farming? Does that sound responsible to you? What farmer would be so careless, even on a day when seed was sown by casting it by hand upon the ground? One would assume that the farmer would be more careful. Yet, he is not and that is rather odd. The reader/listener knows this, and the parable confirms what they know. This is the nature of disruption found in a parable of code and so it is the emphasis of this sermon: it takes the right soil.

Congregations dominated by "good soil" people are those that grow in both number and spirituality, for the good soil expresses the desire for the growth and prosperity experienced within the first-century church. The audience eagerly accepts the gospel message as the three thousand did at Pentecost (Acts 2:38–41). Congregations that grow spiritually and numerically continue to seek after spiritual matters, increasing in the grace and knowledge of the Lord and Savior Jesus Christ (2 Pet 3:18).

Jesus insists we bear some of the responsibility for our growth: "He who has ears to hear, let him hear" (Mark 4:9; Luke 8:8). The word of God is not only located in the mouth of the speaker, but also in the ear of the listener.[143] I am reminded of the familiar statement "you can lead a horse to water, but you can't make him drink." How true that statement is when applied to hearing the message of the gospel. Many will come and sit and attain an attentive posture. They may even express appreciation for "such a fine lesson." They may do all of that and still fail to allow the "seed" to take root in a heart to receive it. We must be soil prepared for planting and carefully tended for a bountiful harvest.

So, who is ready to become the "good soil"? Who is ready to hear the gospel message and accept its saving power? The seed is cast, so which soil will we be? Of course, the choice is obvious, for we must be the soil that will reap a bountiful spiritual harvest. It is clear no other soil will do.

Preaching the Parable of the Sower as Vessel

If the parable of the sower were preached as vessel what would that sermon look like? As a vessel parable, the sower uses comparison and contrast,[144] for the four types of soils are compared and contrasted to how the word proclaimed is accepted by those who will hear it. Hearing the word proclaimed is not an indication of acceptance however, for each soil or hearer represents the willingness to hear, but only one "soil" reaps a bountiful harvest.

The parable tells a story and when preaching utilizes "story" it indicates that something much bigger than the story itself will emerge that is worthy of its telling.[145] The sermon intends to relate something that is captivating, as well as worthwhile. It strives to present the message intended in the parable but do so in a way that motivates the listener to

---

143. Craddock, *Luke*, 111.

144. Long, *Preaching and the Literary Forms*, 99. This is another literary device of a vessel parable. Vessel parables implement the devices of end stress, comparison and contrast, and formula.

145. Lowry, *How Preach a Parable*, 21.

receive the word of God joyfully and faithfully, for receptivity is that which the parable demands.[146] Within this device is the contrast of a lack and abundance of growth. It asks the question, "What does it take to grow?" The sermon will answer the question with a positive proclamation: "Cast the seed upon me; I am ready."

What is allowed to occur after the word is heard becomes significant in the parable. The rhetorical function of a vessel parable is pedagogical and its pedagogy emerges in its presentation the truth contained within the parable.[147] This separates the vessel from the code parable, for the latter seeks to confirm, clarify, and certify what the reader already knows. In preaching the sower its pedagogy arises from an understanding of the soils and their contribution or lack thereof to a bountiful harvest.

If the parable of the sower is preached as vessel or simile, it might look like the following.

"Cast the Seed Upon Me; I Am Ready"

There are certain authors that I like to read. Their books captivate me in ways others do not. The stories they tell take me away from my everyday existence and put me into worlds where I do not live or worlds that exist only as products of a very creative imagination. People like a good story, one that stimulates the imagination and takes the listener on a journey. Jesus took the multitudes on such journeys when he taught them through the use of parables. He told them a story. Perhaps he told them of a spoiled son who ran away from home to find fulfillment elsewhere, only to return home and be honored by his father but spurned by his older brother (Luke 15:11–32). Maybe the story was about a shepherd who had a hundred sheep, but one wandered away and became lost, so the shepherd left the ninety-nine to find the lost sheep (Matt 18:12–14). Jesus might have told a story of a poor, sick beggar and a very wealthy man who both die and find themselves in very different places and circumstances (Luke 16:19–31). In a variety of stories, Jesus engaged his audience in exciting and instructional ways.

Such is the case as Jesus traveled from town to town preaching the gospel of the kingdom of God according to Mark 4 and Luke 8. As he passed through the towns and villages along the way, the people came out and followed him, hoping to hear what he had to say and witness what

---

146. Stein, *Introduction to the Parables*, 113.

147. Long, *Preaching and the Literary Forms*, 97.

he would do. In fact, so many followed and crowded around him at one point that, according to Mark's account of the story, Jesus had to climb into a boat so he could continue to teach them the things concerning the kingdom (Mark 4:1–2).

They followed Jesus because he taught with authority and, so then, was different than the teachers of the law and the Pharisees (Matt 7:28–29). Yet, they also followed him because they were curious about this teacher and prophet who said he spoke the words of God, who he claimed to be his father. So, as they gathered on the shore of the Sea of Galilee, with Jesus sitting in the boat just offshore, he began to speak again. They stood and waited with anticipation. What would he do? What would he tell them?

He told them a parable about a farmer who goes into his field to sow seed (Mark 4:3–8; Luke 8:5–8). The reaction of the audience may have been varied. Some might have had little if any reaction, for they had heard of sowing seed before. Others might have wondered how something exciting and unusual could be drawn from an experience so common and so familiar. After all, the planting of seed was something they all had seen year after year.[148]

Jesus explained that some of the seed fell along the path leading next to or near the field. Being exposed on the ground as it was, the birds soon arrived to eat it (Mark 4:4) and the people passing by walked upon it (Luke 8:5). It could not germinate because it was never long enough on the ground to take root.

Some of the seeds also fell among the rocks. Is this what had been piled up nearby when the field was prepared for planting (Mark 4:5; Luke 8:6)? Some have concluded that the rocky soil echoes the condition of the path, indicating only a thin layer of soil over a bed of rock.[149] Whatever the condition of soil Jesus had in mind, the implication is something unsuitable for planting and germinating seed. It began to quickly grow. However, there was not enough soil in which the plants could take root, so they withered in the hot sun.

Still more of the seed fell on ground that was filled with thorns (Mark 4:7; Luke 8:7). Like weeds will do, the thorns grew with the plants, but began to choke them so they did not bear any grain. Is that not the way it is with weeds? It seems that no matter how hard we try, weeds and grasses seem to grow where we do not want them. They find a way to infiltrate

148. Craddock, *Luke*, 111.

149. Scott, *Hear Then the Parable*, 354.

every flower bed, every field, and wherever one wishes something other than weeds to grow. Is the point, however, on the sower at all, or are we to focus on the seed itself and the soil upon which it falls? Perhaps if we try to make a point of farming techniques, we will miss the point Jesus had in mind as he told the story.

So, the parable is not finished, for to end at this point sends an extremely negative message: the word when it is preached is heard gladly, but never bears fruit. Jesus continues the parable, then, for the rest of the seed fell on the good soil, that part of the field prepared and readied for the planting of seed to produce a harvest (Mark 4:8; Luke 8:8). Now this is more like it, for the farmer saw a harvest befitting the time and effort it would take to produce a crop thirty, sixty, or even a hundred times over (Mark 4:8).

Getting something to grow is sometimes rather difficult. So many things impede success: a lack or abundance of water, improper feeding, too much heat or cold, and any number of other problems. Farmers around the world have faced this problem over and over, sometimes resulting in ruined crops and little or no harvest. Of course, the situation is discouraging.

It is even more discouraging to get the church to grow. So many obstacles arise when efforts are made to cause the spiritual and numerical growth of any congregation. I knew of a young preacher who ministered to a small, struggling congregation in a southern state. This congregation had never been very successful but had somehow maintained its existence through the years. When this young man came onto the scene, he had great expectations for making the congregation grow spiritually and numerically. He had been trained in such things, so he knew he could do it. Yet, in spite of his best efforts, they remained the same, stuck in their rut of complacency, apathy, and habit. He left them discouraged and broken, feeling tremendously inadequate to the task. Churches are supposed to grow!

The parable of the sower offers several reasons why such growth can be difficult. The seed sown along the path, the rocks, and the thorns represent all too much the predicament of many who sit in the pews. They attend most, perhaps all of the Sunday worship assemblies, but several things get in the way of their spiritual transformation. Some of them are like the seed sown along the path. They hear it preached, but they allow the devil's designs to get in the way. Regardless of the power of its proclamation, the gospel message is unheeded because Satan has already tempted them not to allow it to take root. Their attention has been diverted away from their task. Dory, that delightful character in the animated movie *Finding Nemo* is like that.[150] Her attention span and memory are so short she cannot retain a simple point for very long. So, she moves from this to that, never really staying long anywhere at all.

How often does this happen when the word is preached? There are those who willingly hear the word, but they are never brought to salvation, as if the word never had an opportunity to find a place in their hearts. We preach and they appear to listen, perhaps intensely, yet they remain unmoved and unchanged because the power of the word of God is not allowed to take effect.

I recall a man several years ago that attended the activities of the church with his wife, rarely missing an assembly of the congregation. He would sit and listen to the sermon, rarely distracted by anything around him. Each and every time, however, he would leave as if no gospel message had been proclaimed or any plea for salvation had been made. He was the path Jesus had in mind, upon which the seed of God's word had fallen to no avail.

Those like the seed along the path also fail to give their attention very long to any spiritual point. They move from point to point, never accepting the message of the gospel. The devil takes the gospel and its power away as birds would take the seeds lying on the ground. Others in the pews are like the seed sown on the rocks. We live in a world of custom-fitted religion where one can pick and choose what we want as if it were on a cafeteria menu. The gospel is received gladly and anxiously, but faith and conviction do not run very deep. When the challenges of human existence and the realities of the gospel arise—sacrifice and selflessness, for example—what little conviction they have is blown away in the mighty wind of the world.

Being thrilled with the newness of the gospel presentation at first, they soon grow weary of it, and they move on to something else that appears to be new and exciting. There is no conviction because their hearts remain unchanged. There is no dedication because they constantly seek something new. They are offended by the gospel's claims, its restrictions, and its demands. Their lives are their own and no one else, so they wither as a plant in the scorching heat of the world's influence.

Finally, there are those who are like the seed sown among the thorns. In many ways this reflects our modern world better than the pathway and the rocky soil. Notice the seed among the thorns does a bit better at first than the seed in on the pathway and among the rocks. Time has passed

---

150. Stanton, *Finding Nemo*.

between sowing and the stage of growth the seeds have produced. Harvest is approaching and, perhaps, there is some promise of bounty. Yet, all is lost because the seed has germinated among the thorns, and they grow together. Eventually, at some point prior to harvest, the farmer will realize that his crop is lost, even though at one point he saw potential in its production.

There are so many distractions in this day and age that take our time and attention. No one has time for church attendance, to say nothing of participation in spiritual things. There is only just enough time for work, recreation, and the betterment of the physical self. After all, doesn't the Bible say somewhere that one must earn a living? Does Dr. Phil not say we are to make time for our children? Should we not keep doctor's appointments, go to soccer practice, do homework, and a thousand other things that fill each and every day? How can one do those things and still be faithful to church activities as well?

So, the pews are filled with people who want to be in worship, and they seem excited about what the church is trying to accomplish. They sign up for church functions and they volunteer for activities, but they never participate because there is always something else to do. The church may be growing numerically, but it is filled with people distracted by the concerns of the world.

Are we to be discouraged by these people? In truth, we *are* discouraged by them and spend a great deal of time seeking ways to reach them. We try to encourage them with inventive and creative programs, as well as special preaching and teaching events that will motivate them toward participation in spiritual formation. Yet, too often, in spite of all our efforts, they still merely inhabit the pews and rarely seem to improve from their state of apathy. There are preachers and elders all over the nation who stand in quiet resignation for a spiritual version of Murphy's law: the church that is growing is the one you are not in.

The parable, however, insists that there is hope after all. The farmer in the parable sowed seed on four different types of soil, three of which were unsuitable for proper harvest, but the last soil, called the "good" soil, is not only suitable but actually reaps a bountiful harvest. Did you notice a gradual change in the soils and their suitability for germination? As each soil is addressed, there is a gradual increase in suitability: (1) the seed on the path was soon eaten by the birds, (2) the seed on the rocky places grew quickly, but then withered in the sun, (3) the seed among the thorns grew but choked the plants, and (4) the seed on the good soil germinated and produced a bountiful crop.[151] It has been suggested that the sequence gradually directs the listener toward an expectation of success, "actually of overwhelming success, so as to triumph over the three scenes of failure."[152] If this is the case, then the parable intends to move the listener out of a sense of failure and onto a feeling of success.

What then does the parable teach? Maybe Jesus wishes the listener to move toward success, for the sequence mentioned just above moves through concentric circles: from the fringe (path) to the outer rim of soil (rocks), to the carelessly tilled soil (thorns), to the prepared good soil in the midst of the field. In other words, the closer we get to a state of preparedness, the more prepared we are to hear and accept the gospel message.

Perhaps the point of the parable is that in spite of the seemingly insurmountable obstacles that appear to impede our efforts, the gospel of Jesus Christ still yields a bountiful harvest of souls readied for spiritual transformation. Is this a portion of what Jesus had in mind when he spoke of the fields being "ripe for harvest" (John 4:35)? I believe it is, at least in part.

Perhaps the meaning of the parable lies in both views. Spiritual growth comes when we seek the goodness that only comes from having the ears to hear the message of the gospel of Jesus Christ. When one resists the devil (Jas 4:7), seeks a deeper-rooted faith in the Lord (Col 2:7), and puts the kingdom first above the cares of the world (Matt 6:25–33), then spiritual growth emerges from ears ready to receive the word of the Lord.

The parable demands a decision on the part of the listener. This becomes apparent when Jesus proclaims, "He who has ears to hear, let him hear" (Mark 4:9; Luke 8:8). We must take the responsibility to hear the message when it is proclaimed. If the seed is cast upon us, are we ready for it, ready for a bountiful harvest?

God has provided for us the seed. Is the soil prepared and ready? The sower has entered the field and has begun to sow. With God's help, the harvest will be bountiful.

It is our responsibility to say, "Cast the seed upon me; I am ready."

151. Scott, *Hear Then the Parable*, 355.

152. Scott, *Hear Then the Parable*, 355.

CHAPTER 5

THE SPEECHES IN THE BOOK OF ACTS

Examples of Biblical Preaching in the First-Century Church

The book of Acts, also identified as the Acts of the Apostles, is a familiar and often-studied part of the New Testament, offering accounts and events that illuminate the beginning and continuation of the church throughout the first century AD. It is a historical account of the preaching, evangelism, and long reach of the disciples of Jesus Christ and those who would follow their lead as the gospel message was brought into the corners of the known world. Within it are the accounts of those who risked their freedom and their lives for the sake of the message of salvation.

Patrick Schreiner wrote, "The book of Acts offers something unique in the Christian canon. It has no rival in terms of a book spanning so many different lands. Its references to the Spirit far outpace any other work. It functions as a hinge canonically, bridging the Gospels and Epistles. It recounts the birth of the church age, and its content has no parallel in the New Testament."[1] Such uniqueness is why the book of Acts is a popular study within church Bible classes, in courses of study in colleges, universities, and seminaries throughout North America, and throughout the world. In the

---

1. Schreiner, *Mission of the Triune God*, 147.

93

fourth century AD, John Chrysostom called it "a hidden treasure in the New Testament."[2] At this time many within the congregation Chrysostom served were not even aware of the existence of the book of Acts, so he urged them to study it because it "may profit us no less than even the Gospels—so replete is it with Christian wisdom and sound doctrine."[3]

"About half of the Book of Acts consists of speeches, discourses, and letters," wrote Simeon Kistemaker.[4] Merle Bland Dudley is more specific by numbering them at twenty-three.[5] William Willimon places the number of speeches at approximately twenty-eight with the majority coming from Peter and Paul and including the addresses of Christian leaders, apostles, and non-Christian Jews and gentiles.[6]

Willimon asked, "Why did Luke put so much of Acts in the form of speeches?"[7] Unfortunately, he does not definitively answer his question, but he does offer a brief thought. Using Peter's address to the multitude on Pentecost (Acts 2), he noticed that the multitudes' accusation of the drunkenness of the disciples became the impetus behind Peter's address. A pattern is noticed in this event, one that follows fairly uniformly throughout the list of speeches. First, there arose a situation of one or more individuals, usually a crowd, who required some level and amount of information to be given to them regarding a given issue (e.g., the glossolalia of the disciples on Pentecost; the consternation of an Ethiopian seeking to understand the words of the prophet Isaiah; etc.). Second, someone with the knowledge to do so speaks, usually an apostle or a disciple-evangelist (e.g., Peter or Stephen) about the issue in question. Third, an address, speech, or sermon is spoken to the individual or the crowd, seeking to explain further what it is that he or they do not know.

This pattern—event and response—is repeated throughout the book of Acts and reveals the function of the speeches in the unfolding account of preaching and evangelism. This pattern is powerful in its depiction of the speaker-audience-response nature of the book. It allows the reader to be placed within the moment of preaching and to hear the reactions of the crowd. The book of Acts becomes then a testimony of the unbending

2. Kruschwitz and Hughes, *Christian Reflection*, 8.

3. Kruschwitz and Hughes, *Christian Reflection*, 8.

4. Kistemaker, "Speeches in Acts," 31.

5. Dudley, "Speeches in Acts," 1.

6. Willimon, *Acts*, 34.

7. Willimon, *Acts*, 34.

faith and conviction of the disciples of Jesus Christ, bringing the message of salvation and hope into a world that had never heard such things.

Luke's pattern, repeated in some way or the other throughout the book of Acts, reflected a readily familiar rhetorical practice of the classical historians where events, ideas, and issues were interpreted in the delivery of the speech. Willimon admitted that it may, at first, seem to be "a rather unimaginative, prosaic literary convention until we remember how, in our own day, Lincoln's Gettysburg Address did more than open a cemetery—it gave meaning and substance to national cataclysm."[8] Other examples of such a convention of rhetoric would include Martin Luther King, Jr.'s "I Have Dream" speech or Winston Churchill's "Never Was So Much Owed by So Many to So Few" speech.

This chapter is a brief examination of the speeches in the book of Acts. Due to the large number of speeches, twenty-eight or so, a representative sample of speeches, from each of the major contributors—Peter, Stephen, and Paul—will provide the material necessary for such an examination. Emphasis is given to the rhetorical value of the speeches, as well as their theological contributions.

Schreiner made an interesting comment regarding the study of the Bible. "Every book I study in the Bible becomes my new favorite," he began. "That is currently the case with Acts. Spending significant time in any part of Scripture allows one to see the breadth, depth, and beauty of the words from God himself. As Gregory the Great once said, 'Scripture is shallow enough for a child to play in but deep enough for an elephant to drown in.' I like to become an elephant, minus the drowning."[9]

Placing the book of Acts into a specific genre has been the subject of some debate. What is identified today within the New Testament as the book of Acts did not originate with that title.[10] It is the second part in the larger volume called Luke–Acts, coupled, of course, with the Gospel of Luke. When it was separated from Luke's gospel, the need for a title or some other sort of identification became necessary. Tertullian wrote that it was entitled the Memorandum of Luke, while the Muratorian Canon claimed it was identified as the Acts of All of the Apostles,[11] even

---

8. Willimon, *Acts*, 34.

9. Schreiner, *Mission of the Triune God*, 15. Gregory the Great quote from "Letter to Leander," 53.

10. Delbert, *Introduction to the New Testament*, 195.

11. Carson and Moo, *Introduction to the New Testament*, 285.

though the book by no means addresses the activities, speeches, and experiences of all of the apostles. Only the apostles Peter and Paul are recorded. Carson and Moo wrote, "The word 'Acts' (*praxeis*) denoted a recognized genre or subgenre in the ancient world, characterizing books that described the great deeds of people or of cities."[12] "The term Acts stuck, however," wrote John B. Polhill, "and by the third century became the dominant usage."[13] Schreiner observes Acts in comparison to a classic song, where "if Acts is a song, then the Father conducts the ensemble. . . . God the Father orchestrates all actions in Acts toward their prewritten and beautiful end. He has a plan. And it will be accomplished."[14] That is an intriguing thought, for it implies the systematic and orderly way that Acts is arranged in Schreiner's view, of which I agree.

When the dust settles and the smoke clears, the book of Acts is a three-decade history of the church in the first century. Polhill wrote that the majority of scholars refer to the book of Acts as Hellenistic historiography with terms such as "historical monographs," "institutional history," or "political history."[15] Carson and Moo commented, "We visit Jerusalem, Judea, Samaria, Syria, Cyprus, many cities in Asia Minor, Macedonia, Greece, and, finally, Rome. We witness everything from preaching and miracles to jailbreaks and shipwrecks. And while many individuals accompany us on our tour, two are rather constant companions: Peter, who is often with us in Jerusalem, Judea, and Samaria; and Paul, who is our almost constant companion from Syria to Rome."[16]

There are those who resist the book of Acts as a document of history because it does not appear to compare very closely to other historical documents.[17] Spivey and Smith offered the explanation that Luke, and so the book of Acts as well, is not an example of modern historical writing, but is a Gospel or religious writing; in fact, their chapter on the Gospel of Luke is entitled "A Christian Apology."[18] C. H. Talbert preferred to call the book a "Hellenistic 'succession narrative," which "consists of a biography of a founder of a philosophical school, followed by a biography of his successors,"

12. Carson and Moo, *Introduction to the New Testament*, 285.

13. Polhill, "Interpreting the Book of Acts," 391.

14. Schreiner, *Mission of the Triune God*, 29.

15. Schreiner, *Mission of the Triune God*, 391–92.

16. Carson and Moo, *Introduction to the New Testament*, 285–86.

17. Carson and Moo, *Introduction to the New Testament*, 301.

18. Spivey and Smith, *Anatomy of the New Testament*, 139.

citing numerous parallels between Luke's Jesus and the apostles in Acts.[19] Polhill refers to Pervo's suggestion the book of Acts is Hellenistic romance, "a fictional writing that used entertaining stories for purposes of edification," something that would bring "delight" to the readers.[20]

Spivey and Smith wrote that the source of Luke is the Gospel of Mark, as was Matthew, but "[Luke] used his source more critically. Whereas Matthew took over practically all of Mark, Luke used about half. Like Matthew, Luke used the sayings source, Q. In addition, a considerable body of tradition, found only in Luke, makes up the special Lukan tradition."[21]

Did Luke actually write the book of Acts? The second century Muratorian Canon, as well as Irenaeus, believed Luke to be the author.[22] Who was Luke? Paul referred to him as a physician (Col 4:14) and much has been done with that identification of the evangelist to place him more securely as the book's author due to what is seen to be medical language within the text. Polhill wrote that the search for such evidence "has failed," for "Luke did not use technical medical language," but, instead, "wrote in the language of the cultural laity; he wanted to be understood."[23]

As a specific genre, the construction of this part of the book of Acts informs the interplay of the different speeches of Peter and Paul, and how those speeches and their contexts are to be understood. According to Bruce[24] and Hoeck,[25] as well as Kistemaker,[26] the speeches might be divided into four main groups. The first of these groups is "evangelistic" (Acts 8–18). The second group is "deliberative" (19–20). The third main group is "apologetic" (21–26). The fourth group is "hortatory" (26–27).

What are the sources of these speeches in the book of Acts? Kistemaker cites Luke as a source; as an eyewitness to some of the events that lent themselves to the speeches, or as a collector of the information from the eyewitnesses. The question that concerns the student of Acts is whether Luke is giving a truthful presentation in this historical account. Does he accurately

19. Talbert, *Reading Acts*, 3.

20. Polhill, "Interpreting the Book of Acts," 392.

21. Spivey and Smith, *Anatomy of the New Testament*, 139.

22. Spivey and Smith, *Anatomy of the New Testament*, 138.

23. Polhill, "Interpreting the Book of Acts," 392.

24. Bruce, *Speeches in the Acts*, 8–17.

25. Hoeck, "Apostolic Speeches," 2.

26. Kistemaker, "Speeches in Acts," 31.

report the speeches he himself did not hear?[27] We must ask, to be fair to the text, whether Luke's accounting of the speeches was complete, even authentic. Kistemaker asked, "If Luke collected his information from eyewitnesses, does he faithfully reproduce the speeches which they and others make?"[28] These questions are legitimate. Since the speeches are contained within a book attributed to Luke, it is important to establish as clearly and concisely as possible how pristine and complete they are.

Kistemaker responded to his own questions by offering two conclusions. First, if Luke composed "speeches that he places on the lips of the speakers . . . his work, then, is closer to fiction than history."[29] Second, if Luke presents "more or less the exact words the speakers uttered in summarized form . . . [then] he mirrors people as they are with their own peculiarities and characteristics. . . . Luke, then, is both a writer and a historian."[30]

From a linguistic perspective Kistemaker evidently believed Luke to be the collector and reproducer of the speeches the book of Acts contains, rather than a composer of speeches and passing them off as the authentic speeches of Stephen, Peter, or Paul. Luke's recording of the speeches "reflects linguistic peculiarities that show the area and setting in which a dialogue took place. . . . [Luke] reflects the diction, vocabulary, and culture of the area he describes."[31] He cited chapters that depicted Palestine (Acts 1–15), where the Greek "has an Aramaic coloring."[32]

In the second half of the book, chapters 16–28, there is a gentile setting and is written "in fluent Greek that, at times, rivals classical Greek."[33] For example, he wrote that of the sixty-seven times the optative mood occurs in the New Testament, it occurs in the second half of Acts some seventeen times, "from speakers who know Greek well."[34] Luke also uses Semitisms, wrote Kistemaker, such as Jesus' address of Paul on the road to Damascus as *Saoul*, rather than *Saulos* (9:4; 22:7; 26:14; and see 9:17; 22:13). In addition, Governor Festus referred to Nero, emperor of Rome,

27. Kistemaker, "Speeches in Acts," 32.
28. Kistemaker, "Speeches in Acts," 32.
29. Kistemaker, "Speeches in Acts," 33.
30. Kistemaker, "Speeches in Acts," 33.
31. Kistemaker, "Speeches in Acts," 33.
32. Kistemaker, "Speeches in Acts," 33.
33. Kistemaker, "Speeches in Acts," 33.
34. Kistemaker, "Speeches in Acts," 33.

as *ton Sebaston* and *to kurio* (25:25, 26), which, said Kistemaker, "exposes a typical Roman setting."[35]

I entitled this chapter as "another example of biblical preaching." The previous chapter observed the parables of Jesus, their homiletical dynamics, and suggestions on how three of them might be preached according to their literary form. This chapter, however, does not concern itself with how the speeches in Acts might be preached, but with how the speeches are effective examples of biblical preaching themselves. My concerns for this chapter are to examine the speeches in Acts as sermons presented in a variety of settings, to notice literary and rhetorical issues, and to suggest homiletical points that might assist the preacher in his own formation of sermons.

PETER'S SPEECHES IN ACTS

The Choosing of Matthias

Peter emerges not only as a dominant figure within the Gospels and the ministry of Jesus Christ, but as a central leader within the New Testament church in the first century. He was an apostle, of course, as well as a *stulos* ("pillar" or "column") of the church, but he was also a significant speaker within the church.

The first of Peter's speeches in Acts comes at the beginning with the selection of Matthias as the successor to Judas Iscariot (1:16–22). Peter addresses the assembly, "*Andres adelphoi*," or "Men, brothers," an address found elsewhere in the book of Acts (2:29, 37; 7:2; 13:15, 26, 38; 15:7, 13; 22:1; 23:1, 6; 28:17). Acts becomes a clear indication of the concept of *adelphoi* (brothers) found within the New Testament and the first-century church.

Peter's use of David's name and authoritative function is also familiar to students of Acts (2:25, 29, 34; 4:25; 7:45; 13:22; 15:16). Hoeck notices this as an indication of one of many ways Luke makes a clear connection to the Old Testament, as well as in verse 20 where Peter makes "a free rendering" of Ps 69:25 being associated with Judas's fate.[36] Perhaps Peter's immediate follow-up with an application to Ps 109:8 is not quite the free rendering of the context of that part of the Psalter as in the prior example.

---

35. Kistemaker, "Speeches in Acts," 33.

36. Hoeck, "Apostolic Speeches," 4.

Peter's speech in this context makes what is perhaps its primary point with the necessity to choose someone who would be a *marturia*, or "witness," to the resurrection of Jesus Christ. This begins a significant kerygmatic point of Acts, for it is one of eleven occurrences where a form of *martus* is to be found (2:24, 31, 32; 4:2, 10; 33; 5:30; 10:40; 13:30, 33, 34, 37, 41; 17:3, 18, 31, 32; 23:6; 24:15, 21; 26:8, 23). Peter's speech in this context indicates a central testimony of the post-resurrection disciples and that of the early church: the resurrection of Jesus Christ and its significance to a world that would never again be the same.

The Day of Pentecost

Practically on the heels of the Matthias speech is Peter's sermon (speech) on the day of Pentecost (2:14–40). Hoeck incorrectly associates the setting of the Matthias speech and that of Pentecost with the prayer of the apostles gathered around Mary the mother of Jesus (1:13–14). Thus, it is not difficult to imagine how Peter's (Pentecost) speech was imbued with her spirit and sentiments as well. The Marian hermeneutic is of obvious benefit for the instruction of the church's future priests.[37] While the presence of Mary the mother of Jesus was, no doubt, significant and, perhaps, of a level of emotional value, to isolate her as the focus of their act of prayer is assuming what is not indicated within the text. In 1:14 the text reads, "All [the apostles] with one accord were devoting themselves to prayer, together with the women and Mary the mother of Jesus, and his brothers." The devotion to prayer by the disciples is probably better situated on the growing faith of those who had associated with Jesus in a variety of ways, and who had witnessed the evidence of his resurrection. As was stated in regard to the Matthias speech, the resurrection and its implications forms a foundational point of the book of Acts, and that is evidenced very well in the contexts of not only Peter's speeches, but all of the speeches of Acts.

The Pentecost speech of Peter might be divided into two significant parts. First, in 2:14–21 one can see Peter's setting of the moment within the prophecy of Joel 2:28–32. Two things might be seen in this declaration: (1) as the prophecies of Joel were being fulfilled through the events of Jesus' ministry, death, and resurrection, so is a new day of prophecy emerging the faithful would bear witness to the return of the Savior; (2) as the speeches of Acts commence, and so the kerygma of the church of

37. Hoeck, "Apostolic Speeches," 5.

the New Testament as well, a clear recognition of the authority of Scripture established so clearly by Jesus himself now continues to dominant the preaching of his disciples. A second significant part of the Pentecost speech is seen in Peter's connection of Jesus' resurrection to the prophecies of Ps 16:8–11 and Ps 110:1. As Hoeck comments, and on this we can agree, "He is the Lord, pouring out His Spirit."[38]

The communicative value of the Pentecost speech might be seen best in the words used to paint a picture of the speaking event. As the speech begins, the text describes Peter standing (*statheis*) and then lifting up his voice (*epteren ten pronen*) as a Greek orator would do. Such a reference is found elsewhere in Acts (5:20; 11:13; 17:22; 27:21).[39] The picture here is one who would be recognized as getting up to speak, perhaps similar to our modern concept of "having (taking) the floor" or someone standing in a certain spot, such as behind a podium or in front of an audience. Peter's use of judicial rhetoric, along with refutation (2:14–21), indictment (2:22–36), and deliberative rhetoric (2:38-40) rounds out the communicative significance of this speech. Perhaps the greater significance of knowing these patterns is to recognize the deliberative manner in which the apostle spoke. This was not merely someone standing to say a few words, but the act of someone who had something to say.

Peter's Pentecost speech contains a clear Christological kerygma, referring to Jesus as "a man" (*aner*); perhaps a deliberate method of emphasizing the incarnation, as well as the resurrection, punctuated by the declaration, "God raised him up" (2:24a). Hoeck pointed out verses 23–24 where Peter elaborates on the "plan and foreknowledge of God" as Jesus was "delivered up" to be "crucified and killed by the hands of lawless men."[40] As in the Matthias speech, Peter refers to David as an authoritative benchmark of the resurrection of Jesus (2:29–32), following which Jesus was "exalted" and, by implication, enthroned, for David died and was buried, but remained in that condition, bowing, if you will, to the rightful place of the Messiah, Jesus Christ, at the right hand of God (2:34; Ps 110:1).

An interesting Lukan narrative device is introduced here in the book of Acts; that of interruption (7:54; 10:44; 22:22). Peter's Pentecost speech is interrupted by the inquiry of some in the audience who were "cut to the heart" (*katenugesan teo kardian*) and wondered what they were to

---

38. Hoeck, "Apostolic Speeches," 5.

39. Hoeck, "Apostolic Speeches," 5.

40. Hoeck, "Apostolic Speeches," 5.

do (2:37). Peter's reply was for them to repent, be baptized, and receive the gift of the Holy Spirit (2:38), which was not only for them, but for everyone who would do the same (2:39).

In the House of Cornelius

A final speech of Peter to be observed is to the Roman centurion Cornelius (10:28–47). This speech is understood from its context, namely the vision Peter received while on the housetop of Simon the tanner (10:6–16) and the coming of the Holy Spirit upon Cornelius' household toward the conclusion of Peter's speech; perhaps, even another interruption of his words.

Hoeck noticed that this speech emerges as an example of "the form of Petrine kerygma used by the early Church in her earliest approaches to a wider preaching." One cannot wholly agree with Hoeck's assessment of the speech as "purely kerygmatic [rhetoric], offering no indictment in a relatively economic style, i.e., without major elaboration."[41] Peter's speech was certainly kerygmatic, for it expressed the gospel of Jesus' ministry and resurrection. We cannot agree, however, that it was without indictment. While it can be said that the speech does not contain a strong and deliberate expectation of response, Peter nonetheless does indict Cornelius and his household to know what Jesus had said and done "throughout all Judea" (10:37). His statement, "And we are witnesses of all that he did both in the country of the Jews and in Jerusalem" (10:39) became, perhaps, an indictment for Cornelius and his household to know those things as well.

Cornelius' point in bringing Peter to his house must be remembered: "Now therefore we are all here in the presence of God to hear all that you have been commanded by the Lord" (10:33). Peter's speech became a response to that request, and it might be assumed the apostle surpassed Cornelius's expectations. That speech became an indictment for Cornelius and his household to indeed hear all Peter had been commanded to preach. Perhaps Cornelius' use of *prostetagmena* that Peter was to say what he had been "commanded" to say, underestimated Peter's task, as Peter understood it to be. Peter was not merely parroting words commanded of him to say, but he expressed what he felt in his heart. I have believed for some time that this experience was when the light came on in Peter's faith and acceptance of what Jesus had accomplished. His statements, "Truly I understand that God shows no partiality" (10:34), as well as, "And we

41. Hoeck, "Apostolic Speeches," 7.

are witnesses of all that he did" (10:39) seem to express what he had now come to entirely embrace, and so, through his speech, what Cornelius and his household were to embrace as well.

STEPHEN'S SPEECH IN ACTS

Stephen is described just prior to his speech before the Sanhedrin as "a man full of faith and of the Holy Spirit," as well as a man "full of grace and power" (6:5, 8). His efforts to fulfill the calling to "serve tables" (6:2) were cut short upon his detainment by some of the Jewish populace who brought the disciple before the Sanhedrin under false charges (6:9–7:1). His speech emerges as his response to the charges against him.

Kistemaker referred to Stephen's words as the most extensive speech in Acts.[42] Hoeck wrote that the speech, with "the Church's Protomartyr" recounting "the call of Abraham," became "the initial breaking point between the old and the new Israel."[43] The sum of Stephen's speech before the Sanhedrin is one of a narration of the story of God among his people. Stephen began, "The God of glory appeared to our father Abraham when he was in Mesopotamia. . ." (7:2). "The God of glory" statement was perhaps a reference to Ps 29:3 as well as an anticipation of the narrative conclusion in 7:55.[44]

Stephen's speech develops as a series of "telescoping events"[45] that encompass the experiences found in Gen 37–50 and the story of Moses, giving "the narrative a polemical tone."[46] God functions within the unfolding story of the children of Israel that were clearly laid out, emphasizing the iniquities of their ancestors and the righteousness of God toward them, even in his punishment for their wickedness (7:17–43).

Through his use of the phrase *sklerotracheloi kai aperitmetoi kardiais kai tois osin*, "stiff-necked and uncircumcised in heart and ears," Stephen expressed his invective against his audience. Stephen's highly kerygmatic address concluded not with an appeal for change, but an indictment of their spiritual condition; for as their fathers persecuted and killed the righteous of God, so they had done so against "the Righteous One" (7:52),

42. Kistemaker, "Speeches in Acts," 6.

43. Hoeck, "Apostolic Speeches," 6.

44. Hoeck, "Apostolic Speeches," 6.

45. Hoeck, "Apostolic Speeches," 6.

46. Hoeck, "Apostolic Speeches," 6.

a reference, of course, to Jesus Christ. The reaction of the Sanhedrin to such charges was expected and understandable: they had been accused of violating God's law. They gritted their teeth in rage, but Stephen, seemingly unconcerned, only expressed his faith in the final statement of his speech: "Behold, I see the heavens opened, and the Son of Man standing at the right hand of God" (7:56).

Stephen's speech becomes, then, a literal demonstration of Luke's description of his character: a man full of faith and of the Holy Spirit, as well as a man full of grace and power (6:5, 8).

PAUL'S SPEECHES IN ACTS[47]

The Synagogue in Pisidian Antioch

We are introduced to the persecutor Saul in Acts 7:58 and witness his conversion in chapter 9, yet his first speech[48] does not occur until chapter 13 when he speaks to the synagogue in Pisidia (13:16–52). Paul is there with his companion Barnabas, as well as others, and, as was his custom, entered the synagogue. The traditional reading of the Law was heard, and they were asked if they wished to speak. It is at this point that Paul's first speech begins.

This speech, as with most or all of Paul's speeches, focused on the place of Jesus within Jewish history rather than a speech "which tended towards a climax intended to bring repentance."[49] In addition, this speech testifies to the bounty of God's love toward the people he has chosen, so a strong emphasis upon the Old Testament is found. In this way the speech becomes an address of prophecy fulfilled and, so then, the necessity to accept Jesus as the Christ and Son of God through whom the blessings of God would flow.

In the second part of the speech, the apostle appealed to his audience to realize their place in the salvation history of God's people with God as the force behind it, and the place of Jesus within that history (13:26–41). This part of the speech is punctuated by Paul's challenge and admonition to "let it be known" that forgiveness is found only through

---

47. Paul's speeches in the book of Acts are much more extensive than any other list (e.g., Peter). This book observes four of Paul's speeches as a representative sample, excluding all but one of the speeches delivered while in Roman custody.

48. This passage contains two separate speeches of Paul, but to the same audience on two separate Sabbaths. For that reason, I am treating it as one speech.

49. Hoeck, "Apostolic Speeches," 7.

Jesus (13:38), followed by a strong warning to "beware" of falling into the same ill-begotten behavior of their fathers (13:40). The speech receives its climax, perhaps, as Paul outlined the resurrection of Jesus which is able to provide forgiveness and justification that could not be obtained through the law of Moses (13:34–41).

This first speech of Paul had a profound impact on the synagogue, for they invited Paul and his companions to return the following Sabbath to continue, perhaps even reiterate what had been presented to them that day (13:42). Upon their return "the whole city gathered to hear the word of the Lord" (13:44), but the Jews became jealous and contradicted Paul's words (13:45). Paul and his companions announced their disappointment in the Jews: "Since you thrust [the word of God] aside and judge yourselves unworthy of eternal life, behold, we are turning to the Gentiles" (13:46).

On the Areopagus

Paul continued preaching and teaching through Iconium and Lystra, attending a conference in Jerusalem over the question of gentile converts and circumcision (Acts 14, 15). A problem between Paul and Barnabas arose over John Mark, so they separated, and the apostle journeyed through Macedonia and eventually entered Achaia, passing through Thessalonica and Berea, and later arrived in Athens. It was there that Paul's second speech was delivered.

The speech emerges from Paul's distress over the plethora of idols through the city (17:16). He began to reason in the synagogue and the marketplace each day to anyone who would hear his words. Among his audience at a given time were representatives of the two more dominant philosophies at the time, the Stoics and the Epicureans, who claimed that Paul was a *spermologos*, literally "one who picks up seeds" (17:18). Seeing him as "a preacher of foreign divinities" they invited him to speak to them more privately on the Aereopagus, "the Hill of Ares" (17:19). This is a significant development, for it shapes the speech to come. They wanted to hear of this "new teaching"; something intrigued their sense of argumentation (see 17:21) that Paul expressed, which brought "strange things to their ears," and they demanded, "We wish to know therefore what these things mean" (17:20). Paul immediately moved from preaching and teaching to men and women from all levels of their society to the "thinkers" of their time.

It is interesting to note that *statheis*, or "standing," is the same word that is used to describe Peter's Pentecost speech. While *eperen ten phonen*, or "lifting up his voice," is not used to describe Paul's speaking, as with Peter, the inference of the Greek rhetorical style is safely assumed. This is punctuated by him standing "in the midst," or perhaps better, "in the middle" of the Areopagus, an indication of rhetorical intentions.

Paul's address to those on the Areopagus became a challenge to their persistent and overwhelming trust in idols, even to a god that has no identification (17:23). It is on that crucial point that Paul centers his speech: "What therefore you worship as unknown, this I proclaim to you" (17:24). This is interesting, for Paul does not intend to explain the mythology or liturgy of this god with no name, but fully intends to proclaim the validity and legitimacy of the truth they do not know but seek in their attempts to erect an altar in his honor.

Paul's strategy, which is rhetorical in scope, is to reveal, indeed introduce to them the true God they do not know as creator (17:24–26) nor accessible (17:27), utilizing materials familiar to the Greeks; namely, what might be Epimenides's hymn to Zeus—"In him we live and move and have our being"—as well as the poem *Phainomena* by the Stoic poet Aratus—"For we are indeed his offspring."[50] Continuing his challenge to their idolatry and ignorance of the true God, Paul encouraged them by saying, "Being then God's offspring, we ought not to think that the divine being is like gold or silver or stone, an image formed by the art and imagination of man" (17:29).

Stemming from his former declaration to proclaim to them the God they did not know, he offered the caveat, "The times of ignorance God overlooked, but now he commands all people everywhere to repent, because he has fixed a day on which he will judge the world in righteousness by a man whom he has appointed and of this he has given assurance to all by raising him from the dead" (17:30–31). Paul's warning to wise up probably was not lost on the Athenians; regardless of whether they accepted the notion of divine judgment upon the unrepentant, for they must have known the apostle's warning was directed toward them. Regardless, the notion of the resurrection caused some of them to mock him, while some desired to hear more on the subject (17:32). At least four, however, believed and "joined him"; Dionysius the Areopagite and

---

50. Dennis and Grudem, *ESV Study Bible*, 2122.

a woman named Damaris, to name two, while "and others with them" implies at least two more (17:33).

To the Ephesian Elders at Miletus

Paul continued on from Athens to Corinth and, after a period time in Syrian Antioch, traveled to Ephesus where he met with tremendous opposition (18:1–19). Returning to Greece for three months (20:3) he was met with significant opposition once again and set sail, eventually arriving at Troas, where he worshiped with the church there on the first day of the week, where the resurrection of Eutychus occurred (20:6, 7-12). Following these events, Paul traveled on to Assos where he met up with Luke and the others and sailed to Mitylene and finally to Miletus, not desiring to stop in Ephesus (20:13–16).

While in Miletus, Paul sent for the elders of the church in Ephesus. Upon their arrival, he delivered an impassioned appeal (20:17–38). It is significant not only for its pastoral nature, but also because it was the only larger speech to be addressed to Christians.[51] It is its pastoral content that offers "the best prospect of direct comparison between the Paul of Acts and the Paul of the letters."[52] In other words, the portrait of Paul that is seen from the pages of the Epistles is seen in this context as he addresses the elders of the church in Ephesus.

Two literary-critical issues emerge from this speech. First, the identity of its genre, as this was Paul's last public address before he became a prisoner of the Roman government. In this way, wrote Hemer, "it partakes of the character of a will or testament, comprising retrospect and provision for the future . . . a biographical encomium."[53] This point makes the speech a bit odd, for it appears at first to be little more than Pauline statements of self-justification. At first glance, it appears Paul summoned them the forty-four miles[54] to Miletus for him to tell them about himself, his work, and his character. Did the Ephesian elders not know of Paul's contributions, efforts, and abilities? Indeed, they did, but perhaps that was not the point of Paul's seemingly self-centered statements. Paul's

51. Hemer, "Miletus," 77; Dennis and Grudem, *ESV Study Bible*, 2129.
52. Hemer, "Miletus," 77.
53. Hemer, "Miletus," 78.
54. Larkin, *Acts*, 291.

speech is not merely to them, but to a much larger audience where Paul's example becomes an encouragement to do likewise.

Paul's fundamental point in relating his personal story to the elders might be to illustrate his own struggles and accomplishments that were done as a servant of the Lord; Paul's use of *douleuo* "points to the slave-master relationship (Judges 10:16; 1 Sam. 12:20; Lk. 16:13)."[55] Luke's record of the speech isolates two key concepts and ideas: leadership (Acts 22:25–27) and pastoral care (20:31). Luke seems to emphasize both orthopraxy and orthodoxy within Paul's address: the good man that he was and the faith that he displayed.

Second, the purpose of the speech appears to be the *abjuration* of responsibility to the elders of a congregation established by Paul in mission around the known world. This may be directly connected to his description of himself. In other words, as he took responsibility for the church, so should they, reminiscent of his sufferings and struggles written to the church of Corinth: that not only did he suffer so many dangers and persecutions, but he also was responsible for the churches (2 Cor 11:28). Paul evidently is concerned for the future of the Ephesian church. Was this a case of fatherly concern, overly protecting his children from potential future danger, or the apostle's sense of foreboding of imminent trouble ahead?

Paul's encouragement and warning to the Ephesian elders emerge as a list of spiritual and pastoral responsibilities. First, he encouraged them to pay "careful attention to yourselves and to all the flock" (Acts 20:28). Paul is well ahead of the curve for what will become a good leadership technique; that is the task of taking care of oneself as well as those to whom one is a pastoral leader. Second, he reminded them of the source of their authority as well as their responsibility. This point is seen in two parts: (1) that they were made overseers through the power of the Holy Spirit and not by their own authority; (2) they had been placed as leaders of the church that belonged to God. There is a strong sense of stewardship behind Paul's words at this point; they had been given the task of taking care of things that were the possession of God: their owns souls and lives, as well as the church.

The third part of Paul's address aimed directly at their task as *presbuteroi* was both ominous and multifaceted at the same time. Paul warned them of imminent danger, what Paul identified as *lukoi bareis*, or "grievous, oppressive wolves" ("fierce wolves" ESV; "savage wolves" NIV and NKJV), who would take their place within the church in Ephesus and not "spare the

55. Larkin, *Acts*, 293.

flock" (Acts 20:29), which is significant because he had already reminded them that they were to care for that same flock as overseers. Paul's use of *lukoi*, or "wolves," employed connective imagery, for wolves are the predators that attack a flock of sheep. Paul's words imitated the imagery of Jesus as well, who warned the multitude in Matt 7:15, "Beware of false prophets, who come to you in sheep's clothing but inwardly are ravenous wolves [*lukoi arpages*]." In Luke 10:3 Jesus also warned his disciples, "Go your own way: behold, I am sending you out as lambs in the midst of wolves."

That these attacks would occur after Paul's "departure"—he knows that his future is limited—is a statement of Paul's own work among them; they would wait until his authority and personal presence are gone before they would begin to take down the church at Ephesus. The threat would come not just from men on the outside looking in, but also from men who were apart of the church there (Acts 20:30). Does "from among your own selves" ("even from your own number" NIV) in verse 30 indicate a threat from within the congregation as a whole or from within the number of the elders? The *ESV Study Bible* noted that it represented the latter; that not only would threat come in from the outside, but also would arise from among the elders themselves,[56] but such an interpretation is not so certain. The warning must encompass a wider field of vision, and they were to keep watch, as shepherds who watch for the approach of ravenous wolves.

The Speech at the Roman Barracks

After Paul's emotional address to the Ephesian elders at Miletus, he and his companions sailed around the southeast coast of Asia Minor and then made the long journey to the eastern Mediterranean coast, and eventually arrived in Jerusalem (21:1–26). Paul was spotted by Jews from Asia who immediately "laid hands on him" (21:27), accusing the apostle of insurrection against the law and the temple (21:28–29). He was seized and would have been killed had the Roman tribune not been informed and rescued Paul. As they brought Paul up the stair toward the soldiers' barracks, Paul asked the tribune, "May I say something to you?" The tribune was surprised to learn that Paul was not "the Egyptian . . . who recently stirred up a revolt and led the four thousand men of the Assassins out into the wilderness" (21:38). After he had identified himself, he asked permission to speak to the people, which the tribune granted (21:40).

56. Dennis and Grudem, *ESV Study Bible*, 2130.

Luke described Paul "standing on the steps" as he "motioned with his hand to the people" (21:40). *Estos*, "to stand," begins the larger rhetorical movement as Paul was *anabathmon*, "ascending," the steps. In other words, instead of merely standing up and standing straight, Paul stood and ascended a few steps higher. In this position, well in sight of the mob, Paul then *kateseiseo te cheiri to lao*, "motioned with his hand to the people," or, perhaps better, he waved his hand to silence them. All of this becomes a dynamic rhetorical moment. Paul had taken a dominant position, had gotten the attention of the mob, and then created a clear path to effective speech.

So began Paul's speech to the people of Jerusalem, delivered, it can be assumed, to a still hostile mob loudly and vehemently expressing their anger and frustration not only to Paul, but now to the Romans as well. Other speeches of Paul would be delivered in less-than-ideal situations, such as his address before the Sanhedrin (Acts 23:1–6), his apologetic speech before Felix (24:10–21), and before Agrippa II and Bernice (26:1–29). This speech, however, is unique in its extremely hostile environment. The hostility of the mob adds a rhetorical value to the speech perhaps not found by the others. Paul must deliver his speech in a way that calms the crowd.

The result is an address that is similar to the others delivered while a prisoner of Rome, but it is perhaps most similar to the one he delivered before Agrippa II and Bernice (26:1–29). The speech is delivered in Hebrew, probably more correctly understood to have been in Aramaic.[57] It is apologetic in nature, as Paul described his conversion and defended his mission for Jesus Christ. Willimon noticed "four basic units within the body of the speech":[58]

1. A description of Paul's education as a zealous Jew (26:3–5)

2. Paul's encounter with Jesus (26:6–11)

3. Ananias and his help (26:12–16)

4. Paul's vision in the temple (26:17–21)

Rhetorically, Paul's address was brilliantly delivered. First, his use of Aramaic placated the mob for a while, bringing them to relative silence (22:2). Second, he quickly established his Jewish piety[59] through a brief

---

57. Bruce, *Speeches in the Acts*, 23.

58. Willimon, *Acts*, 166.

59. Larkin, *Acts*, 317.

description of his "upbringing and zealotry."[60] Third, Paul then moved the speech to what is rhetorically identified as *probation*, or "body of proof."[61] To do this, the apostle related "four scenes from his conversion and its aftermath":[62]

1. Saul/Paul as a persecutor of Christianity, punctuated by his assertion that he persecuted women and as well as men (22:4), offered as proof of his Jewish zeal (see Phil. 3:6).[63]

2. His divine encounter on the Damascus road, perhaps related to establish, in the sight of witnesses, of this experience.

3. His experiences with Ananias, a man who had a good reputation among the Jews in Damascus, places the event within the realm of both human as well as divine initiative.

4. He testified to his desire for piety and faithful service to God, maintaining his worship (in the temple), but his desire to obey the command of the Lord as well (22:17–21).[64]

So, they listened; that is, until he explained his mission to go to the gentiles (22:21). It is possible he began to lose some of them at his description of the encounter with Jesus on the Damascus road: "I am Jesus of Nazareth, whom you are persecuting" (22:8). In fact, can it be assumed that a building tension is evidenced within the address: the mention of Jesus, his conversion to and preaching within Christianity, and then his mission to take this newfound zeal—the same zeal he showed before his conversion—to the gentiles? I believe it can, but why is this development significant? Rhetorically, it reestablishes the *probation* of his identity as an apostle and disciples of Jesus Christ: what he had done was in obedience to God (could they claim their actions were the same?). What Paul did on the stairs into the Roman barracks was a delivery that was apologetic but was also intended to persuade. This was his modus operandi before the Areopagites (Acts 17) and was the same before the mob in Jerusalem, but instead of converting at least four and earning further discussion in

---

60. Willimon, *Acts*, 166.

61. Larkin, *Acts*, 318.

62. Larkin, *Acts*, 318.

63. Larkin, *Acts*, 318.

64. Larkin, *Acts*, 318.

Athens, it nearly cost him his life in Jerusalem. In so many ways, this speech by Paul stands out among the others.

CONCLUSION

The book of Acts is about the word of God proclaimed, so a majority of the text contains a variety of speeches. Those speeches, for the most part, followed a pattern of thought: (1) a situation that involved one or more individuals requiring some level and amount of information to be given; (2) someone with knowledge spoke to the individual or crowd, usually an apostle or a disciple-evangelist (e.g., Peter or Stephen) about the situation; and (3) the speech sought to explain further what it is that the individual or the crowd did not know.

The speeches in the book of Acts are recognizable by their familiar rhetorical dynamics. These dynamics include the intentional stance and location of the speaker while making the speech, specific words and phrases the speaker might have used, and the way in which the speaker addressed a given issue. All in all, the speeches were made so that the audiences were encouraged to decide.

Why did Luke put so many speeches in Acts? The speeches emerge as true representations of the gospel being taken into the streets, the synagogues, the houses, and even the royal residences of the citizens of the first century. They were the plan of God and the perfect sacrifice of Jesus Christ put into persuasive words. They converted the open-hearted, enraged the closed-minded, and changed the world as they knew it.

CONCLUSION

At the beginning of this book, I asked what preaching is intended to do and then offered an answer from textual, theological, and rhetorical perspectives. There have been hundreds of books before this one that observed what preaching is, so my efforts break no new ground, nor does it offer profound insights never before written. The purpose of this book has been to observe preaching in the light of its source: the Bible. To some, preaching is intended to motivate and encourage. To others, preaching is intended to educate and inform. In the minds of perhaps many preaching is expected to rebuke and exhort. In reality, preaching should be expected to do all of that.

Craddock wrote, "Preaching brings the Scriptures forward as a living voice in the congregation. Biblical texts have a future as well as a past, and preaching seeks to fulfill that future by continuing the conversation of the text into the present."[1] Preaching unites the congregation with the biblical text and the salvation history of God. Robinson calls it, "the event through which God works."[2]

Preaching, however, has not flourished over the past several decades. Instead, it has become unnecessary and archaic in the minds of far too many. That is why the world must be informed on the proper melding of preaching and the biblical text. While that sounds rather obvious, the

1. Craddock, *Preaching*, 27.
2. Robinson, *Biblical Preaching*, 17.

Bible has perhaps been placed on the back burner and replaced with the concerns of oratory, rhetoric, and articulation. The language and thrust of the Bible have become overshadowed by communicative style and the ability of the speaker.

Paul said it well when he wrote to the church in Rome, "For I am not ashamed of the gospel, for it is the power of God for salvation to everyone who believes, to the Jew first and also to the Greek. For in it the righteousness of God is revealed from faith to faith, as it is written, 'The righteous shall live by faith'" (Rom 1:16-17). Paul recognized the immense value of preaching the word of God without compromise or apology because within the Bible is the salvation history of God, the very good news of the promises Jesus Christ through His fulfillment of prophecy and the reality of the church of the New Testament. That church is the one built on the rock-solid foundation of His divinity (Matt 16:18) and is not subject to the machinations of human sensitivities and expectations. In the very same way, the preaching of the church is to reflect Jesus Christ, His will and promises, and the reality of His coming a second and last time to gather all of His disciples to Him for eternity.

One of my favorite songs sung in worship around the world is *The Old Rugged Cross.*[3] The song is, of course, about the cross of Jesus Christ and the singer's reaction to the significance of the cross as "the emblem of suffering shame" that is "so despised by the world," stained with the blood of the Lord. In the song, the singers proclaim their "wondrous attraction" because "the dear Lamb of God left His glory above to bear it to dark Calvary" where Jesus "suffered and died, to pardon and sanctify me." So then, the singers proclaim that to the old, rugged cross they "will ever be true, its shame and reproach gladly bear." Why are the faithful so willing to be true to what the cross of Jesus represents? One day, whenever that day will come, "He'll call me some day to my home far away, where His glory forever I'll share." So, the chorus declares, "So I'll cherish the old rugged cross, till my trophies at last I lay down; I will cling to the old rugged cross and exchange it someday for a crown." Not only is that song so special to me because of Jesus' sacrifice, but because it expresses in a powerful way its incredible message for all to hear, to which the faithful will respond in love and appreciation.

That is what biblical preaching is intended to do: to bring the hearer to a decision based on the undeniable evidence of God's love, authority, and

---

3. George Bennard, "The Old Rugged Cross," in *Songs of Faith and* Praise, Alton H. Howard, ed. (West Monroe, LA: Howard Publishing Co., Inc. 1994), 313.

power contained within His word. The preacher tells the story ("On a hill far away stood an old rugged cross . . . "), explains the significance ("For the dear Lamb of God left His glory above . . . "), then proclaims the disciples' response ("So I'll cherish the old rugged cross . . . "), and then offers the reason for it all ("Then He'll call me someday to my home far away . . . ").

Biblical preaching tells the salvation story of God, proclaiming the details that lie between the emergence of sin, the need of a remedy, and the glorious promise of the Lord for a home in eternity. Biblical preaching does not leave any detail out of the message, but expresses the burden of sin, the decision of all to accept or deny God's scheme of redemption, and the reality of the judgment of the Lord who demands righteousness and justice. Biblical preaching does not alter the truth, pacify the negligent and unbelieving, or remove the need for a decision. It tells the story of the men and women in biblical history who played a role in some way in the unfolding epic saga of heroes, kings and queens, prophets, shepherds, potters, teachers, sages, apostles, and disciples.

As I stated at the very beginning of this book, "Preaching is the presentation, the sharing of the salvation history of God in the Bible. That message is good news, and so then, the gospel. It is powerful, for it is about the word of God, presented by the commission of God to proclaim." Preaching must be biblical, proclaiming without apology love, righteousness, justice, and promises of a loving, judging, eternal God.

BIBLIOGRAPHY

Adam, Peter. Speaking *God's Words: A Practical Theology of Expository Preaching*. Vancouver: Regent College Publishing, 2004.

Bartow, Charles L. *God's Human Speech: A Practical Theology of Proclamation*. Grand Rapids: Eerdmans, 1997.

Best, John W., and James V. Kahn. *Research in Education, Seventh Edition*. Boston: Allyn and Bacon, 1993.

Black, C. Clifton. "Four Stations en Route to a Parabolic Homiletic." *Interpretation* 54 (October 2000) 386–97.

Blomberg, Craig L. *Interpreting the Parables*. Downers Grove: InterVarsity, 1990.

———. "Preaching the Parables: Preserving Three Main Points." *Perspectives in Religious Studies* 11 (Spring 1984) 31–44.

Bond, L. Susan. "Taming the Parable: The Problem of Parable as Substitute Myth." *Homiletic* 25.1 (Summer 2000) 1–12.

Brice, Alexander Balmain. *The Parabolic Teaching of Christ: A Systematic and Critical Study of the Parables of Our Lord*. Madrid: Hardpress, 2012.

Brouwer, Wayne. "Reframing Life: Preaching That Changes People's Perspectives." *Preaching* (March–April 1998) 30–33.

Brown, Sally A. "Preaching as Spiritual Formation." *Journal for Preachers* 21 (Lent 1998) 26–30.

Bruce, F. F. *The Speeches in the Acts of the Apostles*. London: Tyndale, 1942.

Brueggeman, Walter. *Hope within History*. Atlanta: John Knox, 1987.

Buttrick, David. *Speaking Parables: A Homiletic Guide*. Louisville: Westminster John Knox Press, 2000.

Campbell, Charles L. *Preaching Jesus: New Directions for Homiletics in Hans Frei's Postliberal Theology*. Grand Rapids: Eerdmans, 1997.

Carey, George. "The Spiritual Life of the Preacher." *Preaching* (July–August 1997) 2–7.

Carson, D. A. *The Expositor's Bible Commentary with the NIV: Matthew 13–28*. Grand Rapids: Zondervan Publishing House, 1995.

Carson, D. A. and Moo, Douglas J. *An Introduction to the New Testament.* Nottingham, England: Apollos, 2005.

Cavendish, Lucy. "Atkinson Has Been There and He's Done That." The Scotsman, 2005. https://web.archive.org/web/20061018071947/http://living.scotsman.com/index. cfm?id=2323922005.

Craddock, Fred B. *As One without Authority.* Des Peres, MO: Chalice, 2001.

———. *Luke: Interpretation; A Bible Commentary for Teaching and Preaching.* Louisville: John Knox, 1990.

———. *Preaching.* Nashville: Abingdon, 1985.

Crossan, John Dominic. *In Parables: The Challenge of the Historical Jesus.* Sonoma, CA: Poleridge, 1992.

Decaro, Peter. "2.3: The Roman Republic." LibreTexts: Social Sciences, n.d. https:// socialsci.libretexts.org/Bookshelves/Communication/Public_Speaking/ Public_Speaking_(The_Public_Speaking_Project)/02:_Origins_of_Public_ Speaking/2.03:_The_Roman_Republic.

Delbert, Burkett. *An Introduction to the New Testament and the Origins of Christianity.* Cambridge: Cambridge University Press, 2001.

Dennis, Lane, and Wayne Grudem, eds. *ESV Study Bible.* Wheaton, IL: Crossway, 2001.

Dodd, C. H. *The Parables of the Kingdom.* London: Collins-Fontana, 1961.

Donahue, John R. *The Gospel in Parable: Metaphor, Narrative, and Theology in the Synoptic Gospels.* Philadelphia: Fortress, 1988.

———. "Jesus as the Parable of God in the Gospel of Mark." *Interpretation* 32 (1978) 369–86.

Dudley, Merle Bland. "The Speeches in Acts," *Evangelical Quarterly* 50.3 (July–September 1978) 147–55. https://biblicalstudies.org.uk/pdf/eq/1978-3_147.pdf.

Duduit, Michael. "Preaching and Pain: An Interview with Ron Mehl." Preaching, 1995. https://www.preaching.com/articles/preaching-and-pain-an-interview-with-ron-mehl/.

Elliott, Mark Berger. *Creative Styles of Preaching.* Louisville: Westminster John Knox, 2000.

Emmerich, Roland, dir. *The Day after Tomorrow.* 20th Century Fox and Centropolis Entertainment, 2004.

English, Donald. *The Message of Mark: the Mystery of Faith.* Downers Grove: InterVarsity, 1992.

Eslinger, Richard L. "Preaching the Parables and the Main Idea." *The Perkins School of Theology Journal* 31 (Fall 1983) 24–32.

Fant, Clyde. "What Can Preaching Do?" *Faith and Mission* 3 (Fall 1985) 3–11.

Fleer, David and Dave Bland, eds. *Preaching From Luke/Acts.* Abilene, TX: Abilene Christian University Press, 2000.

Glen, J. Stanley. *The Parables of Conflict in Luke.* Philadelphia: Westminster, 1962.

Graves, Mike. *The Sermon as Symphony: Preaching the Literary Forms of the New Testament.* Valley Forge: Judson, 1997.

Green, Michael. *The Message of Matthew.* Grand Rapids: IVP Academic, 2020.

Greidanus, Sidney. *The Modern Preacher and the Ancient Text.* Grand Rapids: Eerdmans, 1988.

Gregory the Great. "Letter to Leander." In *Moral Reflections on the Book of Job*, translated by Brian Kerns, 53. Collegeville, MN: Liturgical.

Griffiths, Jonathan. *Preaching in the New Testament.* Downer's Grove, IL: InterVarsity, 2017.

Gushee, David P., and Walter C. Jackson, eds. *Preparing for Christian Ministry.* Grand Rapids: Baker, 1998.

Haddon, Robinson. *Biblical Preaching: The Development and Delivery of Expository Messages.* Grand Rapids: Baker, 1980.

Harper, Steve. "Wesley's Sermons as Spiritual Formation Documents." *Methodist History* 26 (April 1988) 131–38.

Hemer, Colin J. "The Speeches of Acts I: Miletus." Tyndale Bulletin 40.1 (1989) 77–85.

———. "The Speeches of Acts II: The Areopagus Address." Tyndale Bulletin 40.2 (1989) 239–59.

Henry, Robert T. *The Golden Age of Preaching: Men Who Moved the Masses.* Lincoln, NE: iUniverse, 2005.

"Herald." Merriam-Webster, n.d. https://www.merriam-webster.com/dictionary/herald.

Hethcock, William. "The Sermon as an Educational Event." *Sewanee Theological Review* 38 (1994) 21–38.

Hoeck, Andreas. "The Apostolic Speeches in Acts and Seminary Teaching Methods." Saint Paul Seminary, 2011. https://saintpaulseminary.org/wp-content/uploads/2018/11/Hoeck_QI_2011_Aposto.pdf.

Hughes, Robert G. "Preaching the Parables." In *The Promise and Practice of Biblical Theology*, edited by John Reumann, 157–70. Minneapolis: Augsburg, 1991.

Hunter, A. M. "Interpreting the Parables: The Gospel in Parables." Part 2. *Interpretation* 14 (April 1960) 167–85.

———. "Interpreting the Parables: The Gospel in Parables." Part 3. *Interpretation* 14 (July 1960) 315–32.

———. "Interpreting the Parables: The Interpreter and the Parables." Part 1. *Interpretation* 14 (January 1960) 70–84.

———. "Interpreting the Parables: The Proclamation of the Kingdom." Part 4. *Interpretation* 14 (October 1960) 440–54.

Jensen, Richard A. *Telling the Story.* Minneapolis: Augsburg, 1980.

Jeremias, Joachim. *The Parables of Jesus.* New York: Charles Scribner's Sons, 1972.

Jewell, Elizabeth J., and Frank Abate. *Oxford Illustrated American Dictionary.* London: Oxford University Press, 1998.

Jones, Peter Rhea. "Preaching on the Parable Genre." *Review And Expositor* 94 (Spring 1997) 231–45.

Kistemaker, Simon J. "The Speeches in Acts." *Criswell Theological Review* 5.1 (1990) 31–34.

Koessler, John. "A View from the Pew: Lessons about Preaching from the Other Side of the Pulpit." *Preaching* (July–August 1996) 20–22.

Kruschwitz, Robert B., and Heather Hughes, eds. *Christian Reflection: A Series in Faith and Ethics.* Waco, TX: Baylor University Institute for Faith and Learning, 2015.

Larkin, William J., Jr. *Acts.* IVP New Testament Commentary Series. Edited by Grant Osborne. Downers Grove, IL: IVP Academic, 1995.

Larsen, David L. *Telling the Old, Old Story: The Art of Narrative Preaching.* Grand Rapids: Kregel, 1995.

Liefeld, Walter L. *New Testament Exposition: From Text to Sermon.* Grand Rapids: Zondervan, 1984.

Lindbeck, George A. *The Nature of Doctrine: Religion and Theology in a Postliberal Age.* Philadelphia: Westminster, 1984.

Lischer, Richard. *Theories of Preaching: Selected Readings in the Homiletical Tradition.* Durham, NC: Labyrinth, 1987.

Long, Thomas G. *Preaching and the Literary Forms of the Bible.* Philadelphia: Fortress, 1989.

———. *The Witness of Preaching.* Louisville: Westminster John Knox, 1989.

Loscalzo, Craig A. *Evangelistic Preaching That Connects: Guidance in Shaping Fresh and Appealing Sermons.* Downers Grove, IL: InterVarsity, 1995.

Lowry, Eugene L. *The Homiletical Plot.* Atlanta: John Knox Press, 1989.

———. *How to Preach a Parable: Designs for Narrative Sermons.* Nashville: Abingdon, 1989.

———. "Regarding Homiletic Distortions: A Response to 'Taming the Parable: The Problem of Parable as Substitute Myth.'" *Homiletic* 25.2 (Winter 2000) 3–7.

———. *The Sermon: Dancing the Edge of Mystery.* Nashville: Abingdon, 1997.

Marberry, Jenny. "Students Make Big Discovery." *The Morning News,* Jan 23, 2003. http://www.nwamorningnews.com/pdfarchive/2003/january/23.

Maxwell, John. "Leading through Preaching: An Interview with John Maxwell." *Preaching* (January–February 1998) 14–18.

McGrath, Alister E. *The Genesis of Doctrine: A Study in the Foundations of Doctrinal Criticism.* Oxford: Basil Blackwell, 1990.

Nichols, Bruce, ed. *American Heritage Dictionary of the English Language.* 5th ed. Boston: Houghton Mifflin Harcourt, 2016.

Noyce, Gaylord. *The Minister as Moral Counselor.* Nashville: Abingdon, 1989.

O'Day, Gail R. "Bible and Sermon: Conversation between Text and Preacher." In *Sharing Heaven's Music,* edited by James Earl Massey and Barry L. Callen, 69–81. Nashville: Abingdon, 1995.

Palmer, Gary. *Toward a Theory of Cultural Linguistics.* Austin: University of Texas Press, 1996.

Perrin, Norman. *Jesus and the Language of the Kingdom: Symbol and Metaphor in New Testament Interpretation.* Philadelphia: Fortress, 1976.

Polhill, John B. "Interpreting the Book of Acts." In *Interpreting the New Testament: Essays on Methods and Issues,* edited by David Alan Black and David S. Dockery, 391–411. Nashville: Broadman and Holman, 2001.

Ramsey, W. M. *St. Paul the Traveller and the Roman Citizen.* Grand Rapids: Baker, 1962.

Rainer, Tom. *Surprising Insights among the Unchurched.* Grand Rapids: Zondervan, 2008.

Resner, Andre. *Preacher and Cross: Person and Message in Theology and Rhetoric.* Grand Rapids: Eerdmans, 1999.

Ricoeur, Paul. "Listening to the Parables of Jesus." *Criterion* 13 (Spring 1974) 18–22.

Schreiner, Patrick. *The Mission of the Triune God: A Theology of Acts.* New Testament Theology. Edited by Patrick R. Scheiner and Brian S. Rosner. Wheaton, IL: Crossway, 2022.

Scott, Bernard Brandon. *Hear Then the Parable: A Commentary on the Parables of Jesus.* Minneapolis: Fortress, 1989.

Skeat, T. C. "The Last Chapter in the History of the Codex Sinaiticus." *Novum testamentum* 42.4 (2000) 313–15.

Spivey, Robert A., and D. Moody Smith Jr. *Anatomy of the New Testament.* London: Macmillan, 1969.

Stagg, Frank. "Luke's Theological Use of Parables." *Review And Expositor* 94 (Spring 1997) 215–29.

Stanton, Andrew, dir. *Finding Nemo*. Walt Disney Pictures and Pixar Animation Studios, 2003.

Steele, Les L. *On the Way: A Practical Theology of Christian Formation*. Grand Rapids: Baker, 1990.

Stein, Robert H. *An Introduction to the Parables of Jesus*. Philadelphia: Westminster, 1981.

Street, James L. "Preaching and Discerning Human Need." *Preaching* (March–April 1995) 31–32.

Talbert, C. H. *Reading Acts: A Literary and Theological Commentary on the Acts of the Apostles*. New York: Crossroad, 1997.

———. *Reading Luke: A Literary and Theological Commentary on the Third Gospel*. New York: Crossroad, 1992.

TeSelle, Sallie McFague. "Parable, Metaphor, and Theology." *Journal of the American Academy of Religion* 42 (December 1974) 630–45.

Thielman, Frank. "Preaching the Parables." *Preaching* 8 (July–August 1992) 27–31.

Thomsen, Mark. "A Parabolic Theology for Preaching." *Dialog* 19 (Summer 1980) 199–204.

Tozer, James. "Preaching to Reluctant Pilgrims." *Preaching* 9 (May–June 1994) 21–24.

Trench, Richard Chenevix. *Note on the Parables of Our Lord*. Grand Rapids: Baker, 1948.

Via, Dan Otto. *The Parables: Their Literary and Existential Dimension*. Philadelphia: Fortress, 1967.

Wardlaw, Don M., ed. *Preaching Biblically*. Philadelphia: Westminster, 1983.

Wilken, Robert L. "In Defense of Allegory." *Modern Theology* 14 (April 1998) 197–212.

Willimon, William H. *Acts: Interpretation; A Bible Commentary for Teaching and Preaching*. Atlanta: John Knox, 1988.

———. *Peculiar Speech: Preaching to the Baptized*. Grand Rapids: Eerdmans, 1992.

Wilson, Paul Scott. *The Four Pages of the Sermon: A Guide to Practical Preaching*. Nashville: Abingdon, 1999.